CEREMONIES
IN
DARK OLD MEN

LONNE ELDER III

CEREMONIES
IN
DARK OLD MEN

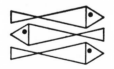

THE NOONDAY PRESS
FARRAR, STRAUS AND GIROUX
NEW YORK

The Noonday Press
A division of Farrar, Straus and Giroux
19 Union Square West, New York 10003

Copyright © 1965, 1969 by Lonne Elder III
All rights reserved
Published in Canada by HarperCollins*CanadaLtd*
Printed in the United States of America
Library of Congress catalog card number: 70-87212
Designed by Sheila Lynch
First published simultaneously in hardcover and
paperback by Farrar, Straus and Giroux in 1969
First Noonday paperback edition, 1997

This play is dedicated to
My son, David Dubois Elder
My wife, Judith Ann
To the memory of my life's teacher,
Dr. William E. B. Dubois
To the memory of Dr. Martin Luther King
To the Negro Ensemble Company

CEREMONIES
IN
DARK OLD MEN

———◆◆———

The Negro Ensemble Company production of *Ceremonies in Dark Old Men* opened at the St. Marks Playhouse, New York City, on February 4, 1969, with the following cast:

MR. RUSSELL B. PARKER	DOUGLAS TURNER
MR. WILLIAM JENKINS	ARTHUR FRENCH
THEOPOLIS PARKER	WILLIAM JAY
BOBBY PARKER	DAVID DOWNING
ADELE ELOISE PARKER	ROSALIND CASH
BLUE HAVEN	SAMUAL BLUE, JR.
YOUNG GIRL	JUDYANN ELDER

Directed by Edmund Cambridge

Early spring, about 4:30 in the afternoon, now.

A small, poverty-stricken barbershop on 126th Street between Seventh and Lenox avenues, Harlem, U.S.A.

There is only one barber's throne in this barbershop. There is a not too lengthy mirror along the wall, and a high, broad shelf in the immediate area of the throne. There are two decks of shelves of equal width projecting just below the main shelf. These shelves are covered by small, sliding panels. On the far left corner of the shop is the street door, and on the far right corner is a door leading to a back room. Just to the right of the door, flush against the wall, is a card table and two chairs. Farther right is a clothes rack. Against the wall to the far left of the shop, near the door, are four chairs lined up uniformly.

The back room is like any back room in a poverty-stricken barbershop. It has an old refrigerator, an even older antique-type desk, and a medium-size bed. On the far right is a short flight of stairs leading up. A unique thing about this room: a door to stairs coming up from a small basement.

The action of the play takes place in the barbershop and the back room.

ACT ONE

SCENE ONE

---◄♦►---

As the curtain rises, MR. RUSSELL B. PARKER *is seated in the single barber's throne, reading the* Daily News. *He is in his early or middle fifties. He rises nervously, moves to the window, and peers out, his right hand over his eyebrows. He returns to the chair and continues to read. After checking his watch, he rises again and moves to the window for another look. Finally he sees the right person coming and moves to the door to open it.* MR. WILLIAM JENKINS *enters: early fifties, well dressed in a complete suit of clothes, and carrying a newspaper under his arm.*

MR. PARKER

Where have you been?

MR. JENKINS

Whatcha mean? You know where I was.

9

MR. PARKER

You want to play the game or not?

MR. JENKINS

That's what I came here for.

MR. PARKER

(*Slides open a panel in the counter.*) I wanted to get in at least three games before Adele got home, but this way we'll be lucky if we get in one.

MR. JENKINS

Stop complaining and get the board out—I'll beat you, and that will be that.

MR. PARKER

I can do without your bragging. (*Pulls out a checkerboard and a small can, quickly places them on the table, then shakes up the can.*) Close your eyes and take a man.

MR. JENKINS

(*Closing his eyes.*) You never learn. (*Reaches into the can and pulls out a checker.*) It's red.

MR. PARKER

All right, I get the black. (*Sits at the table and rushes to set up his men.*) Get your men down, Jenkins!

MR. JENKINS

(*Sits.*) Aw, man, take it easy, the checkers ain't gon' run away! (*Setting his men up.*) If you could play the game I wouldn't mind it—but you can't play! —Your move.

MR. PARKER

I'll start here—I just don't want Adele to catch us here playing checkers. She gave me and the boys a notice last week that we had to get jobs or get out of the house.

MR. JENKINS

Don't you think it's about time you got a job? In the five years I've been knowing you, I can count the heads of hair you done cut in this shop on one hand.

MR. PARKER

This shop is gon' work yet; I know it can. Just give me one more year and you'll see . . . Going out to get a job ain't gon' solve nothing—all it's gon' do is create a lot of bad feelings with everybody. I can't work! I don't know how to! (*Moves checker.*)

MR. JENKINS

I bet if all your children were living far from you like mine, you'd know how to. That's one thing I don't understand about you, Parker. How long do you expect your daughter to go on supporting you and those two boys?

11

MR. PARKER

I don't expect that! I just want some time until I can straighten things out. My dear Doris understood that. She understood me like a book. (*Makes another move.*)

MR. JENKINS

You mean to tell me your wife enjoyed working for you?

MR. PARKER

Of course she didn't, but she never worried me. You been married, Jenkins: you know what happens to a man when a woman worries him all the time, and that's what Adele been doing, worrying my head off! (*Makes another move.*)

MR. JENKINS

Whatcha gon' do about it?

MR. PARKER

I'm gon' get tough, evil and bad. That's the only sign a woman gets from a man. (*Makes move.*)

(THEOPOLIS PARKER *enters briskly from street. He is in his twenties, of medium height, and has a lean, solid physique. His younger brother* BOBBY *follows, carrying a huge paper bag whose contents are heavy and fragile.*)

THEO

That's the way I like to hear you talk, Pop, but she's gon'

be walking through that door soon, and I wants to see how tough you gon' be.

MR. PARKER

Leave me alone, boy.

THEO

Pop, we got six more days. You got to do something!

MR. PARKER

I'll do it when the time comes.

THEO

Pop, the time is *now*.

MR. PARKER

And right now I am playing a game of checkers with Mr. Jenkins, so leave me alone!

THEO

All right—don't say I didn't warn you when she locks us out of the house!

(THEO *and* BOBBY *rush through the back room.* BOBBY *places the brown bag in the old refrigerator as they dart up the stairs leading to the apartment.* PARKER *makes another move.*)

13

MR. PARKER

You're trapped, Jenkins!

(*Pause.*)

MR. JENKINS

(*Pondering.*) Hmmmmmm . . . It looks that way, don't
it?

MR. PARKER

(*Moves to the door.*) While you're moaning over the
board, I'll just make a little check to see if Adele is coming . . . Don't cheat now! (*He backs toward the window, watching that his adversary does not cheat. He
quickly looks out the window.*) Uh-uh! It's Adele! She's
in the middle of the block, talking to Miss Thomas!
(*Rushes to take out a towel and spreads it over the
checkerboard.*) Come on, man! (*Drags* MR. JENKINS
by the arm toward the back room.)

MR. JENKINS

What are you doing, Parker!

MR. PARKER

You gon' have to hide out in the back room, 'cause if
Adele comes in here and sees you, she'll think that we
been playing checkers all day!

14

MR. JENKINS

I don't care about that!

MR. PARKER

You want to finish the game, don't you?

MR. JENKINS

Yeah, but—

MR. PARKER

All you have to do, Jenks, is lay low for a minute, that's
all. She'll stop in and ask me something about getting a
job, I'll tell her I got a good line on one, and then she'll
go on upstairs. There won't be nobody left here but you
and me. Whatcha say, Jenks?

MR. JENKINS

(*Pause.*)
All right, I'll do it. I don't like it, but I'll do it, and you
better not mention this to nobody, you hear!

MR. PARKER

Not a single soul in this world will know but you and me.

MR. JENKINS

(*Moves just inside the room and stands.*) This is the most
ridiculous thing I ever heard of, hiding in somebody's
back room just to finish up a checker game.

15

MR. PARKER
Stop fighting it, man!

MR. JENKINS
All right!

MR. PARKER
Not there!

MR. JENKINS
What in the hell is it now!

MR. PARKER
You've got to get under the bed!

MR. JENKINS
No, I'm not gettin' under nobody's bed!

MR. PARKER
Now look . . . Adele never goes through the front way. She comes through the shop and the back room, up the basement stairs to the apartment. Now you want her to catch you hiding in there, looking like a fool?

MR. JENKINS
No, I can take myself out of here and go home!

MR. PARKER
(*Pushes* JENKINS *over to the table and uncovers the*

checkerboard.) Look at this! Now you just take a good look at this board! (*Releases him.*)

MR. JENKINS

I'm looking, so what?

MR. PARKER

So what? I got you and you know it! There ain't no way in the world you'll ever get out of that little trap I got you in. *And it's your move.* How many years we been playing against each other?

MR. JENKINS

Three.

MR. PARKER

Never won a game from you in all that time, have I?

MR. JENKINS

That ain't the half of it. You ain't gon' win one either.

MR. PARKER

Now that I finally got you, that's easy talk, comin' from a running man. All right, go on. Run. (*Moves away.*)

MR. JENKINS

Go on, hell! All I gotta do is put my king here, give you this jump here, move this man over there, and you're dead!

17

MR. PARKER

(*Turns to him.*) Try me then. Try me, or are you scared at last I'm gon' beat you?

MR. JENKINS

I can't do it now, there ain't enough time!

MR. PARKER

(*Strutting like a sport.*) Run, rabbit, run . . .

MR. JENKINS

All right! I'll get under the bed. But I swear, Parker, I'm gon' beat you silly! (*They move into the back room.*)

MR. PARKER

Hurry it up then. We ain't got much time.

(*As* MR. PARKER *struggles to help* MR. JENKINS *get under the bed in the back room,* ADELE *comes in from the street. She is in her late twenties, well dressed in conventional New York office attire. She is carrying a smart-looking handbag and a manila envelope. She stops near the table on which checkerboard is hidden under towel.* MR. PARKER *enters from the back room.*)

MR. PARKER
Hi, honey.

(She doesn't answer, instead busies herself putting minor things in order.)

ADELE

You looked for work today?

MR. PARKER

All morning . . .

(Pause.)

ADELE

No luck in the morning, and so you played checkers all afternoon.

MR. PARKER

No, I've been working on a few ideas of mine. My birthday comes up the tenth of the month, and I plan to celebrate it with an idea to shake up this whole neighborhood, and then I'm gon' really go to the country!

ADELE

Don't go to the country—go to work, huh? *(Moves toward back room.)* Oh, God, I'm tired!

MR. PARKER

(Rushing to get her away from bed.) Come on and let me take you upstairs. I know you must've had yourself

a real tough day at the office . . . and you can forget about cooking supper and all of that stuff.

ADELE

(*Breaks away, moves back into shop toward counter.*) Thank you, but I've already given myself the privilege of not cooking your supper tonight.

MR. PARKER

You did?

ADELE

The way I figure it, you should have my dinner waiting for me.

MR. PARKER

But I don't know how to cook.

ADELE

(*Turns sharply.*) You can learn.

MR. PARKER

Now look, Adele, if you got something on your mind, say it, 'cause you know damn well I ain't doin' no cooking.

ADELE

(*Pause.*)
All right, I will. A thought came to me today as it does every day, and I'm damn tired of thinking about it—

MR. PARKER

What?

ADELE

—and that is, I've been down at that motor-license bu-
reau so long, sometimes I forget the reasons I ever took
the job in the first place.

MR. PARKER

Now look, everybody knows you quit college and came
home to help your mama out. Everybody knows it! What
you want me to do? Write some prayers to you?

(*The two boys enter the back room from upstairs.*)

ADELE

I just want you to get a job!

(*The boys step into shop and stand apart from each other.*)

BOBBY

Hey, Adele.

ADELE

Well! From what cave did you fellows crawl out of? I
didn't know you hung around barbershops . . . Want
a haircut, boys?

21

THEO

For your information, this is the first time we been in this barbershop today. We been upstairs thinking.

ADELE

With what?

THEO

With our *minds,* baby!

ADELE

If the two of you found that house upstairs so attractive to keep you in it all day, then I can think of only three things: the telephone, the bed, and the kitchen.

BOBBY

The kitchen, that's it: we been washing dishes all day!

ADELE

I don't like that, Bobby!

THEO

And I don't like your attitude!

ADELE

Do you like it when I go out of here every morning to work?

THEO

There you go again with that same old tired talk: work!
Mama understood about us, I don't know why you gotta
give everybody a hard time . . .

ADELE

That was one of Mama's troubles: understanding everybody.

THEO

Now don't start that junk with me!

ADELE

I have got to start that, *Mr. Theopolis Parker!*

MR. PARKER

Hold on now, there's no need for all this . . . Can't we
settle this later on, Adele . . .

ADELE

We settle it now. You got six days left, so you gotta do
something, and quick. I got a man coming here tomorrow
to change the locks on the door. So for the little time you
have left, you'll have to come by me to enter this house.

THEO

Who gives you the right to do that?

ADELE

Me, Adele Eloise Parker, black, over twenty-one, and the only working person in this house!

(*Pause.*)

I am not going to let the three of you drive me into the grave the way you did Mama. And if you really want to know how I feel about that, I'll tell you: Mama killed herself because there was no kind of order in this house. There was nothing but her old-fashion love for a bum like you, Theo—and this one (*points to* BOBBY) who's got nothing better to do with his time but to shoplift every time he walks into a department store. And you, Daddy, you and those fanciful stories you're always ready to tell, and all the talk of the good old days when you were the big vaudeville star, of hitting the numbers big. How? How, Daddy? The money you spent on the numbers you got from Mama . . . In a way, you let Mama make a bum out of you—you let her kill herself!

MR. PARKER

That's a terrible thing to say, Adele, and I'm not going to let you put that off on me!

ADELE

But the fact remains that in the seven years you've been in this barbershop you haven't earned enough money to buy two hot dogs! Most of your time is spent playing checkers with that damn Mr. Jenkins.

THEO

(*Breaks in.*) Why don't you get married or something! We don't need you—Pop is here, it's HIS HOUSE!

ADELE

You're lucky I don't get married and—

THEO

Nobody wants you, baby!

ADELE

(THEO's *remark stops her for a moment. She resettles herself.*) All right, you just let someone ask me, and I'll leave you with *Pop,* to starve with Pop. Or, there's another way: why don't the three of you just leave right now and try making it on your own? Why don't we try that!

MR. PARKER

What about my shop?

ADELE

Since I'm the one that has to pay the extra forty dollars a month for you to keep this place, there's going to be no more shop. It was a bad investment and the whole of Harlem knows it!

25

MR. PARKER

(*Grabbing her by the arm, in desperation.*) I'm fifty-four years old!

ADELE

(*Pulling away.*) Don't touch me!

MR. PARKER

You go ahead and do what you want, but I'm not leaving this shop! (*Crosses away from her.*)

ADELE

Can't you understand, Father? I can't go on forever supporting three grown men! *That ain't right!*

(*Long pause.*)

MR. PARKER

(*Shaken by her remarks.*) No, it's not right—it's not right at all.

ADELE

—It's going to be *you* or *me.*

BOBBY

(*After a pause.*) I'll do what I can, Adele.

ADELE

You'll do *more* than you can.

26

BOBBY

I'll do more than I can.

ADELE

Is that all right by you, Mr. Theopolis?

THEO

Yes.

(*Pause.*)

ADELE

That's fine. Out of this house tomorrow morning—before I leave here, or with me—suit your choice. And don't look so mournful (*gathers up her belongings at the shelf*), smile. You're going to be happier than you think, earning a living for a change. (*Moves briskly through the back room and up the stairs.*)

BOBBY

You do look pretty bad, Theo. A job might be just the thing for you.

(MR. JENKINS *comes rushing from the bed into the shop.*)

MR. PARKER

Jenkins! I plumb forgot—

27

MR. JENKINS

I let you make a fool out of me, Parker!

MR. PARKER

We can still play!

MR. JENKINS

(*Gathering his jacket and coat.*) We can't play nothing,
I'm going home where I belong!

MR. PARKER

Okay, okay, I'll come over to your place tonight.

MR. JENKINS

That's the only way. I ain't gon' have my feelings hurt by
that daughter of yours.

MR. PARKER

I'll see you tonight—about eight.

MR. JENKINS

(*At the door.*) And, Parker, tell me something?

MR. PARKER

Yeah, what, Jenks?

MR. JENKINS

Are you positively sure Adele is your daughter?

MR. PARKER

Get out of here! (MR. JENKINS *rushes out.*) Now what made him ask a silly question like that?

THEO

I think he was trying to tell you that you ain't supposed to be taking all that stuff from Adele.

BOBBY

Yeah, Pop, he's right.

(MR. PARKER *starts putting his checker set together.*)

THEO

(*To* BOBBY.) I don't know what you talking about—you had your chance a few minutes ago, but all you did was poke your eyes at me and nod your head like a fool.

BOBBY

I don't see why you gotta make such a big thing out of her taking charge. Somebody's gotta do it. I think she's right!

THEO

I know what she's up to. She wants us to get jobs so she can fix up the house like she always wanted it, and then it's gon' happen.

BOBBY

What's that?

29

THEO

She gon' get married to some konkhead out on the Avenue, and then she gon' throw us out the door.

BOBBY

She wouldn't do that.

THEO

She wouldn't, huh? Put yourself in her place. She's busting thirty wide open. *Thirty years old*—that's a lot of years for a broad that's not married.

BOBBY

I never thought of it that way . . .

THEO

(*In half confidence.*) And you know something else, Pop? I sneaked and peeped at her bank book, and you know what she got saved?

MR. PARKER and BOBBY

(*Simultaneously, turning their heads.*) How much!?

THEO

Two thousand two hundred and sixty-five dollars!

BOBBY

WHAT!!!

MR. PARKER

I don't believe it!

THEO

You better—and don't let her hand you that stuff about
how she been sacrificing all these years for the house. The
only way she could've saved up that kind of money was
by staying right here!

MR. PARKER

Well, I'll be damned—two thousand dollars!

THEO

She better watch out is all I gotta say, 'cause I know some
guys out there on that Avenue who don't do nothing but
sit around all day figuring out ways to beat working girls
out of their savings.

MR. PARKER

You oughta know, 'cause you're one of them yourself.
The way I figure it, Theo, anybody that can handle you
the way she did a few minutes ago can very well take care
of themselves. (*He occupies himself putting checkers and
board away and cleaning up.*)

THEO

That's mighty big talk coming from you, after the way she
treated you.

MR. PARKER

Lay off me, boy.

THEO

You going out to look for a job?

MR. PARKER

I'm giving it some serious thought.

THEO

Well, I'm not. I ain't wasting myself on no low, dirty, dead-end job. I got my paintings to think about.

BOBBY

Do you really think you're some kind of painter or something?

THEO

You've seen them.

BOBBY

Yeah, but how would I know?

THEO

(*Rushes into the back room, takes paintings from behind the refrigerator.*) All right, look at 'em.

BOBBY

Don't bring that stuff in here to me—show it to Pop!

(THEO *holds up two ghastly, inept paintings to his brother.* MR. PARKER, *sweeping the floor, pays no attention.*)

THEO

Look at it! Now tell me what you see.

BOBBY

Nothing.

THEO

You've got to see something—even an idiot has impressions.

BOBBY

I ain't no idiot.

THEO

All right, fool then.

BOBBY

Now look, you better stop throwing them words "fool" and "idiot" at me any time you feel like it. I'm gon' be one more fool, and then my fist is gonna land right upside your head!

THEO

Take it easy now—I tell you what: try to see something.

33

BOBBY

Try?

THEO

Yeah, close your eyes and really try.

BOBBY

(*Closes his eyes.*) Okay, I'm trying, but I don't know how I'm gon' see anything with my eyes closed!

THEO

Well, open them!

BOBBY

They open.

THEO

Now tell me what you see.

BOBBY

I see paint.

THEO

I know you see paint, stupid.

BOBBY

(*Slaps him ferociously across the face.*) Now I told you about that! Every time you call me out of my name, you get hit!

THEO

You'll never understand!

BOBBY

All I know is that a picture is supposed to be pretty, but I'm sorry, that mess you got there is downright ugly!

THEO

You're hopeless.—You understand this, don't you, Pop? (*Holding the painting for him to see.*)

MR. PARKER

(*Not looking at the painting.*) Don't ask me—I don't know nothing about no painting.

THEO

You were an artist once.

MR. PARKER

That was a different kind.

THEO

Didn't you ever go out on the stage with a new thing inside of you? One of them nights when you just didn't want to do that ol' soft-shoe routine? You knew you had to do it—after all, it was your job—but when you did it, you gave it a little bite here, a little acid there, and still, with all that, they laughed at you anyway. Didn't that ever happen to you?

MR. PARKER

More than once . . . But you're BSn', boy, and you
know it. You been something new every year since
you quit school. First you was going to be a racing-car
driver, then a airplane pilot, then a office big shot, and
now it's a painter. As smart a boy as you is, you should've
stayed in school, but who do you think you're fooling
with them pictures?—It all boils down to one thing: you
don't want to work. But I'll tell you something, Theo:
time done run out on you. Adele's not playing, so you
might as well put all that junk and paint away.

THEO

Who the hell is Adele? You're my father, you're the man
of the house.

MR. PARKER

True, and that's what I intend to be, but until I get a job,
I'm gon' play it cool.

THEO

You're going to let her push you out into the streets to
hustle up a job. You're an old man. You ain't used to
working, it might kill you.

MR. PARKER

Yeah, but what kind of leg do I have to stand on if she
puts me out in the street?

THEO

She's bluffing!

MR. PARKER

A buddy of mine who was in this same kind of fix told me exactly what you just said. Well, the last time I saw him, he was standing on the corner of Eighth Avenue and 125th Street at four o'clock in the morning, twenty-degree weather, in nothing but his drawers, mumbling to himself, "I could've sworn she was bluffing!"

THEO

Hey, Pop! Let me put it to you this way: if none of us come up with anything in that two-week deadline she gave us—none of us, you hear me?

MR. PARKER

I hear you and that's just about all.

THEO

Don't you get the point? That's three of us—you, me, and Bobby. What she gon' do? Throw the three of us out in the street? I tell you, she ain't gon' do that!

MR. PARKER

If you want to take that chance, that's your business, but don't try to make me take it with you. Anyway, it ain't right that she has to work for three grown men. It just ain't right.

THEO

Mama did it for you.

MR. PARKER

(*Sharply.*) That was different. She was my wife. She knew things about me you will never know. We oughtn' talk about her at all.

THEO

I'm sorry, Pop, but ever since Mama's funeral I've been thinking. Mama was the hardest-working person I ever knew, and it killed her! Is that what I'm supposed to do? No, that's not it, I know it's not. You know what I've been doing? I've been talking to some people, to a very important person right here in Harlem, and I told him about this big idea of mine—

MR. PARKER

You're loaded with ideas, boy—*bad ideas!* (*Puts broom away.*)

THEO

WHY DON'T YOU LISTEN TO WHAT I HAVE TO SAY!

MR. PARKER

Listen to you for what? Another con game you got up your sleeve because your sister's got fed up with you lying around this house all day while she's knocking herself out. You're pulling the same damn thing on me you did with those ugly paintings of yours a few minutes ago.

THEO

Okay, I can't paint. So I was jiving, but now I got something I really want to do—something I got to do!

MR. PARKER

If you're making a point, Theo, you've gotta be smarter than you're doing to get it through to me.

THEO

(*Goes to back room, opens refrigerator, and takes out brown-paper bag, then comes back into the shop.*) Pop, I got something here to show how smart I really am. (*Lifts an old jug out of the bag.*) Check this out, Pop! Check it out!

MR. PARKER

What is it?

THEO

Whiskey—corn whiskey—you want some?

MR. PARKER

(*Hovers.*) Well, I'll try a little bit of it out, but we better not let Adele see us.

THEO

(*Starts unscrewing cork from jug.*) That girl sure puts a scare in you, Pop, and I remember when you wouldn't take no stuff off Mama, Adele, or nobody.

MR. PARKER

God is the only person I fear.

THEO

(*Stops unscrewing the jug.*) God! Damn, you're all alike!

MR. PARKER

What are you talking about, boy?

THEO

You, the way Mama was—ask you any question you can't answer, and you throw that Bible stuff at us.

MR. PARKER

I don't get you.

THEO

For instance, let me ask you about the black man's oppressions, and you'll tell me about some small nation in the East rising one day to rule the world. Ask you about pain and dying, and you say, "God wills it." . . . Fear?— and you'll tell me about Daniel, and how Daniel wasn't scared of them lions. Am I right or wrong?

40

MR. PARKER

It's all in the book and you can't dispute it.

THEO

You wanta bet? If that nation in the East ever do rise, how can I be sure they won't be worse than the jokers we got running things now?—Nobody but nobody wills me to pain and dying, not if I can do something about it. That goes for John, Peter, Mary, J.C., the whole bunch of 'em! And as for ol' Daniel: sure, Daniel didn't care nothing about them lions—*but them lions didn't give a damn about him either! They tore him into a million pieces!*

MR. PARKER

That's a lie! That's an ungodly, unholy lie! (*Takes his Bible from the shelf.*) And I'll prove it!

THEO

What lie?

MR. PARKER

(*Moving from the counter, thumbing through Bible.*) You and those bastard ideas of yours. Here, here it is! (*Reading from Bible.*) "And when he came near unto the den to Daniel, he cried with a pained voice; The King spoke and said to Daniel: 'O Daniel, servant of the living God, is thy God, whom thou servest continually, able to deliver thee from the lions?' Then said Daniel unto the King: 'O

41

King, live forever! My God hath sent his angel, and hath shut the lions' mouths, and they have not hurt me; for as much as before him innocence was found in me, and also before thee, O King, have I done no hurt.' Then was the King exceeding glad, and commanded that they should take Daniel up out of the den. So Daniel was taken up out of the den, and no manner of hurt was found upon him, because he trusted his God!!!" (*Slams the book closed, triumphant.*)

THEO

Hollywood, Pop, Hollywood!

MR. PARKER

Damn you! How I ever brought something like you into this world, I'll never know! You're no damn good! Sin! That's who your belief is! Sin and corruption! With you, it's nothing but women! Whiskey! Women! Whiskey! (*While he is carrying on,* THEO *pours out a glass of corn and puts it in* MR. PARKER'S *hand.*) Women! Whiskey! (*Takes a taste.*) Whisk— Where did you get this from? (*Sits on throne.*)

THEO

(*Slapping* BOBBY'S *hand.*) I knew you'd get the message, Pop—I just knew it!

MR. PARKER

Why, boy, this is the greatest corn I ever tasted!

BOBBY

And Theo puts that stuff together like he was born to be a whiskey maker!

MR. PARKER

Where did you learn to make corn like this?

THEO

Don't you remember? You taught me.

MR. PARKER

By George, I did! Why, you weren't no more'n nine years old—

THEO

Eight. Let's have another one. (*Pours another for* PARKER.) Drink up. Here's to ol' Daniel. You got to admit one thing—he had a whole lot of heart!

MR. PARKER

(*Drinks up and puts his hand out again.*) Another one, please . . .

THEO

(*Pouring.*) Anything you say, Pop! *You're the boss of this house!*

MR. PARKER

Now that's the truth if you ever spoke it. (*Drinks up.*)

43

Whew! This is good! (*Putting his glass out again, slightly tipsy.*)

THEO

About this idea of mine, Pop: well, it's got something to do with this corn.

MR. PARKER

(*Drinks up.*) Wow! Boy, people oughta pay you to make this stuff.

THEO

Well, that's what I kinda had in mind. I tested some of it out the other day, and I was told this corn liquor could start a revolution—that is, if I wanted to start one. I let a preacher taste some, and he asked me to make him a whole keg for him.

MR. PARKER

(*Pauses. Then, in a sudden change of mood.*) God! Damnit!

BOBBY

What's wrong, Pop?

MR. PARKER

I miss her, boy, I tell you, I miss her! Was it really God's will?

THEO

Don't you believe that—*don't you ever believe that!*

MR. PARKER

But I think, boy—I think hard!

THEO

That's all right. We think hard too. We got it from you.
Ain't that right, Bobby?

BOBBY

Yeah.

MR. PARKER

(*Pause.*)
You know something? That woman was the first woman
I ever got close to—your mama . . .

BOBBY

How old were you?

MR. PARKER

Twenty.

BOBBY

Aw, come on, Pop!

MR. PARKER

May God wipe me away from this earth . . .

THEO

Twenty years old and you had never touched a woman?
You must've been in bad shape.

MR. PARKER

I'll tell you about it.

THEO

Here he goes with another one of his famous stories!

MR. PARKER

I can always go on upstairs, you know.

THEO

No, Pop, we want to hear it.

MR. PARKER

Well, I was working in this circus in Tampa, Florida—
your mother's hometown. You remember Bob Shepard—
well, we had this little dance routine of ours we used to
do a sample of outside the tent. One day we was out there
doing one of our numbers, when right in the middle of the
number I spied this fine, foxy-looking thing, blinking her
eyes at me. 'Course ol' Bob kept saying it was him she was
looking at, but I knew it was *me*—'cause if there was one
thing that was my specialty, it was a fine-looking woman.

THEO

You live twenty years of you life not getting anywhere near a woman, and all of a sudden they become *your specialty?*

MR. PARKER

Yeah, being that—

THEO

Being that you had never had a woman for all them terrible years, naturally it was on your mind all the time.

MR. PARKER

That's right.

THEO

And it being on your mind so much, you sorta became a specialist on women?

MR. PARKER

Right again.

THEO

(*Laughs.*) I don't know. But I guess you got a point there!

MR. PARKER

You want to hear this or not!?

47

BOBBY

Yeah, go on, Pop. *I'm* listening.

MR. PARKER

Well, while I was standing on the back of the platform, I motions to her with my hand to kinda move around to the side of the stand, so I could talk to 'er. She strolled 'round to the side, stood there for a while, and you know what? Ol' Bob wouldn't let me get a word in edgewise. But you know what she told him; she said Mister, you talk like a fool! (*All laugh.*)

BOBBY

That was Mama, all right.

MR. PARKER

So I asked her if she would like to meet me after the circus closed down. When I got off that night, sure enough, she was waiting for me. We walked up to the main section of town, off to the side of the road, 'cause we had a hard rain that day and the road was full of muddy little ponds. I got to talking to her and telling her funny stories and she would laugh—boy, I'm telling you that woman could laugh!

THEO

That was your technique, huh? Keep 'em laughing!

MR. PARKER

Believe it or not, it worked—'cause she let me kiss her. I kissed her under this big ol' pecan tree. She could kiss too. When that woman kissed me, somethin' grabbed me so hard and shook me so, I fell flat on my back into a big puddle of water! *And that woman killed herself laughing!*

(*Pause.*)

I married her two weeks later.

THEO

And then you started making up for lost time. I'm glad you did, Pop—'cause if you hadn't, I wouldn't be here today.

MR. PARKER

If I know you, you'd have made some kind of arrangement.

BOBBY

What happened after that?

MR. PARKER

We just lived and had fun—and children too, that part you know about. We lived bad and we lived good—and then my legs got wobbly, and my feet got heavy, I lost my feeling, and everything just stayed as it was.

(*Pause.*)

I only wish I had been as good a haircutter as I was a dancer. Maybe she wouldn't have had to work so hard. She might be living today.

THEO

Forget it, Pop—it's all in the gone by. Come on, you need another drink. (*Pouring.*)

MR. PARKER

Get me to talking about them old days. It hurts, I tell you, it—

THEO

Pop, you have got to stop thinking about those things. We've got work to do!

MR. PARKER

You said you had an idea . . .

THEO

Yes—you see, Pop, this idea has to do with Harlem. It has to do with the preservation of Harlem. That's what it's all about. So I went to see this leader, and I spoke to him about it. He thought it was great and said he would pay me to use it!

MR. PARKER

Who wants to preserve this dump! Tear it down, is what
I say!

THEO

But this is a different kind of preserving. Preserve it for
black men—preserve it for men like you, me, and Bobby.
That's what it's all about.

MR. PARKER

That sounds good.

THEO

Of course I told this leader, I couldn't promise to do
anything until I had spoken to my father. I said, after
straightening everything out with you I would make
arrangements for the two of you to meet.

MR. PARKER

Meet him for what?

THEO

For making money! For business! *This man knows how to
put people in business!*

MR. PARKER

All right, I'll meet him. What's his name?

THEO

—But first you gotta have a showdown with Adele and put her in her place once and for all.

MR. PARKER

Now wait just a minute. You didn't say Adele would have anything to do with this.

THEO

Pop, this man can't be dealing with men who let women rule them. Pop, you've got to tell that girl off or we can't call ourselves men!

MR. PARKER

(*Pause.*)

All right. If she don't like it, that's too bad. Whatever you have in mind for us to do with this leader of yours, we'll do it.

THEO

Now that's the way I like to hear my old man talk! Take a drink, Pop! (*Starts popping his fingers and moves dancing about the room.*)

We're gonna show 'em now
We're gonna show 'em how
All over
This ol' Harlem Town!

(THEO *and* BOBBY *start making rhythmic scat sounds with their lips as they dance around the floor.*) —Come on, Pop, show us how you used to cut one of them things!

BOBBY

(*Dancing.*) This is how he did it!

THEO

Nawwww, that's not it. He did it like this!

MR. PARKER

(*Rising.*) No, no! Neither one of you got it! Speed up that riff a little bit . . . (*The two boys speed up the riff, singing, stomping their feet, clapping their hands. Humped over,* MR. PARKER *looks down on the floor concentrating.*) Faster! (*They speed it up more.*)

THEO

Come on now, Pop—let 'er loose!

MR. PARKER

Give me time . . .

BOBBY

Let that man have some time!

(MR. PARKER *breaks into his dance.*)

53

THEO
 Come on, Pop, take it with you!

BOBBY
 Work, Pop!

THEO
 DOWNTOWN!

(MR. PARKER *does a coasting "camel walk."*)

BOBBY
 NOW BRING IT ON BACK UPTOWN!

(MR. PARKER *really breaks loose: a rapid series of complicated dance steps.*)

THEO
 YEAHHHHHHH!

BOBBY
 That's what I'm talkin' about!

(ADELE *enters, stops at the entrance to the shop, observes the scene, bemused.* PARKER, *glimpsing her first, in one motion abruptly stops dancing and reaches for the broom.* BOBBY *looks for something to busy himself with.* THEO *just stares.*)

54

ADELE

Supper's ready, fellows!

CURTAIN

SCENE TWO

Six days later. Late afternoon.

BOBBY *is seated in the barber's throne, munching on a sand-wich.* THEO *enters from the front of the shop.*

THEO

Did Pop get back yet?

(BOBBY *shrugs shoulders.*)

THEO

You eating again? Damn. (*Calling upstairs.*) Pop! (*No answer.* THEO *checks his watch, steps back into shop, looks through window, then crosses to* BOBBY *and snatches the sandwich from his mouth.*) You eat too damn much!

BOBBY

What the fuck you do that for?

THEO

(*Handing the sandwich back.*) 'Cause you always got a mouth full of peanut butter and jelly!

BOBBY

I'm hungry! And let me tell you something: don't you *ever* snatch any food from my mouth again.

THEO

You'll hit me—you don't care nothing about your brother. One of these days, I'm gon' hit back.

BOBBY

Nigger! The day you swing your hand at me, you'll draw back a nub.

THEO

You see! That's exactly what I mean. Now when Blue gets here tonight, I don't want you talking like that, or else you gon' blow the whole deal.

BOBBY

I know how to act. I don't need no lessons from you.

THEO

Good. I got a job for you.

58

BOBBY

A job? Shit!

THEO

Don't get knocked out now—it ain't no real job. I just
want you to jump over to Smith's on 125th Street and
pick me up a portable typewriter.

BOBBY

Typewriter—for what?

THEO

Don't ask questions, just go and get it.

BOBBY

Them typewriters cost a lotta money.

THEO

You ain't gon' use money.

BOBBY

You mean—

THEO

—I mean you walk in there and take one.

BOBBY

Naw, you don't mean I walk into nowhere and take nothing!

THEO

Now, Bobby.

BOBBY

No!

THEO

Aw, come on, Bobby. You the one been bragging about
how good you are, how you can walk into any store and
get anything you wanted, provided it was not too heavy to
carry out.

BOBBY

I ain't gon' do it!

THEO

You know what day it is?

BOBBY

Thursday.

THEO

That's right. Thursday, May 10th.

BOBBY

What's that suppose to mean, Thieves' Convention on
125th Street?

THEO

It's Pop's birthday!

BOBBY

I didn't know he was still having them.

THEO

Well, let me tell you something: Adele remembered it and she's planning on busting into this shop tonight with a birthday cake to surprise him.

BOBBY

She suppose to be throwing us out today. That don't make no sense with her buying him a birthday cake.

THEO

He's been looking for work, I guess she changed her mind about him. Maybe it's gon' be just me and you that goes.

BOBBY

(*Pause.*)
What's he gon' type?

THEO

Them lies he's always telling—like the one about how he met Mama. Pop can tell some of the greatest lies you ever heard of and you know how he's always talking about writing them down.

BOBBY

Pop don't know nothing 'bout writing—specially no type-writing!

THEO

(*Takes out his father's notebook.*) Oh no? take a look at this. (*Hands book to* BOBBY.) All he has to do is put it down on paper the way he tells it. Who knows, somebody might get interested in it for television or movies, and we can make ourselves some money, and besides, I kinda think he would get a real charge out of you thinking about him that way—don't you?

BOBBY

(*Pause.*)
Well, ain't no use in lettin' you go over there, gettin' your-self in jail with them old clumsy fingers of yours.

THEO

Good boy, Bobby! (MR. PARKER *enters the shop.*) Hey, Pop! Did you get that thing straightened out with Adele yet?

MR. PARKER
What?

THEO
Adele?

MR. PARKER

Oh, yeah, I'm gon' take care of that right away. (*Shoves* BOBBY *out of throne and sits.*)

THEO

Where you been all day?

(BOBBY *moves into back room.*)

MR. PARKER

Downtown, seeing about some jobs.

THEO

You sure don't care much about yourself.

MR. PARKER

I can agree with you on that, because lookin' for a job can really hurt a man. I was interviewed five times today, and I could've shot every last one of them interviewers—the white ones and the colored ones too. I don't know if I can take any more of this.

THEO

Yeah, looking for a job can be very low-grading to a man, and it gets worse after you get the job. Anyway, I'm glad you got back here on time, or you would've missed your appointment. (*No response from* PARKER.) Now don't tell me you don't remember! The man, the man that's suppose to come here and tell you how life in Harlem can be profitable.

MR. PARKER

(*Steps out of throne, edging toward back room.*) Oh, that.

THEO

(*Following him.*) Oh, that—my foot! Today is the day we're suppose to come up with those jobs, and you ain't said one word to Adele about it—not one single word! All you do is waste your time looking for work! Now that don't make no sense at all, Pop, and you know it.

MR. PARKER

Look, son. Let me go upstairs now and tell her about all the disappointments I suffered today, soften her up a bit, and then I'll come on back down here to meet your man. I promise, you won't have to worry about me going downtown any more—not after what I went through to-day. And I certainly ain't giving up my shop for nobody! (*Exits upstairs.*)

THEO

(*Turns to* BOBBY, *who's at the mirror.*) Now that's the way I like to hear my old man talk! Hey, baby, don't forget that thing. It's late, we ain't got much time.

BOBBY

All right!

(*A jet-black-complexioned young man comes in. He is dressed all in blue and wears sunglasses. He carries a gold-top cane and a large salesman's valise. He stops just inside the door.*)

THEO

Blue, baby!

BLUE

Am I late?

THEO

No, my father just walked in the door. He's upstairs now, but he'll be right back down in a few minutes. Let me take your things. (*Takes* BLUE's *cane and valise.*) Sit down, man, while I fix you a drink. (*Places* BLUE's *things on the table and moves into back room.* BOBBY *enters shop.*)

BLUE

Hey, Bobby. How's the stores been treating you?

BOBBY

I'm planning on retiring next year. (*Laughs.*)

THEO

(*Returning with jug and two glasses. Moves to the table and pours.*) I was thinking, Blue—we can't let my old man know about our "piano brigade." I know he ain't going for that, but we can fix it where he will never know a thing.

BLUE

You know your father better than I do. (*Takes a drink.*)

BOBBY

What's the "piano brigade"?

THEO

Blue here has the best thieves and store burglars in this part of town, and we plan to work on those businesses over on 125th Street until they run the insurance companies out of business.

BOBBY

You mean breaking into people's stores at night and taking their stuff?

THEO

That's right, but not the way you do it. We'll be organized, we'll be revolutionary.

BOBBY

If the police catch you, they ain't gon' care what you is, and if Pop ever finds out, the police gon' seem like church girls! (*Slips out the front door.*)

THEO

(*After him.*) You just remember that the only crime you'll ever commit is the one you get caught at!

(*Pause.*)

Which reminds me, Blue—I don't want Bobby to be a part of that "piano brigade."

BLUE

If that's the way you want it, that's the way it shall be, Theo. How's your sister?

THEO

You mean Adele?

BLUE

You got a sister named Mary or something?

THEO

What's this with Adele?

BLUE

I want to know, how are you going to get along with her, selling bootleg whiskey in this place?

THEO

This is not her place, it's my father's. And once he puts

his okay on the deal, that's it. What kind of house do you think we're living in, where we gon' let some woman tell us what to do? Come here, let me show you something. (*Moves into back room.* BLUE *follows.*) How you like it—ain't it something?

BLUE

(*Standing in doorway.*) It's a back room.

THEO

Yeah, I know. But I have some great plans for reshaping it by knocking down this wall, and putting—

BLUE

Like I said, it's a back room. All I wanta know is, will it do the job? It's a good room. You'll do great with that good-tasting corn of yours. You're going to be so busy here, you're going to grow to hate this place—you might not have any time for your love life, Theopolis!

THEO

(*Laughing.*) Don't you worry about that—I can manage my sex life!

BLUE

Sex! Who's talking about sex? You surprise me, Theo. Everyone's been telling me about how you got so much heart, how you so deep. I sit and talk to you about life, and you don't know the difference between sex and love.

THEO

Is it that important?

BLUE

Yes, it is, ol' buddy, if you want to hang out with me, and you do want to hang out with me, don't you?

THEO

That depends—

BLUE

It depends upon you knowing that sex's got nothing to do with anything but you and some woman laying up in some funky bed, pumping and sweating your life away all for one glad moment—you hear that, *one moment!*

THEO

I'll take that moment!

BLUE

With every woman you've had?

THEO

One out of a hundred!

BLUE

(*Laughing, and moving back into shop.*) One out of a hundred! All that sweat! All that pumping and grinding for the sake of one little dead minute out of a hundred hours!

(MR. PARKER *comes in from upstairs.*)

THEO
(*Pause. Stopping* PARKER.) Pop, you know who this is?

MR. PARKER
I can't see him.

THEO
This is Blue!

MR. PARKER
Blue who?

THEO
The man I was telling you about . . . *Mr. Blue Haven.*

MR. PARKER
(*Extends his hand to shake* BLUE's.) Please to make your acquaintance, Mr. Haven.

BLUE
(*Shaking* MR. PARKER's *hand.*) Same to you, Mr. Parker.

THEO
You sure you don't know who Blue Haven is, Pop?

MR. PARKER

I'm sorry, but I truly don't know you, Mr. Haven. If you're a celebrity, you must accept my apology. You see, since I got out of the business, I don't read the *Variety* any more.

THEO

I'm not talking about a celebrity.

MR. PARKER

Oh, no?

THEO

He's the leader!

MR. PARKER

Ohhhhh!

THEO

Right here in Harlem.

MR. PARKER

Where else he gon' be but in Harlem? We got more leaders within ten square blocks of this barbershop than they got liars down in City Hall. That's why you dressed up that way, huh, boy? So people can pick you out of a crowded room?

THEO

Pop, this is serious!

MR. PARKER

All right, go on, don't get carried away—there are some
things I don't catch on to right away, Mr. Blue.

THEO

Well, get to this: I got to thinking the other day when
Adele busted in here shoving everybody around—I was
thinking about this barbershop, and I said to myself:
Pop's gon' lose this shop if he don't start making himself
some money.

MR. PARKER

Now tell me something I don't know. (*Sits on throne.*)

THEO

Here I go. What would you say if I were to tell you that
Blue here can make it possible for you to have a thriving
business going on, right here in this shop, for twenty-four
hours a day?

MR. PARKER

What is he—some kind of hair grower!

THEO

Even if you don't cut but one head of hair a week!

MR. PARKER

Do I look like a fool to you?

THEO

(*Holds up his jug.*) Selling this!

MR. PARKER

(*Pause.*)

Well, well, well. I knew it was something like that. I didn't exactly know what it was, but I knew it was something. And I don't want to hear it!

THEO

Pop, you've always been a man to listen—even when you didn't agree, even when I was wrong, you listened! That's the kind of man you are! You—

MR. PARKER

Okay, okay, I'm listening!

THEO

(*Pause.*)

Tell him who you are, Blue.

BLUE

I am the Prime Minister of the Harlem De-Colonization Association.

MR. PARKER
(*Pause.*)
Some kind of organization?

BLUE
Yes.

MR. PARKER
(*As an aside, almost under his breath.*) They got all kinds
of committees in Harlem. What was that name again,
"De"?

THEO
De-Colo-ni-zation! Which means that Harlem is owned
and operated by Mr. You-Know-Who. Let me get this
stuff—we gon' show you something . . . (*Moves to the
table and opens* BLUE'*s valise.*)

BLUE
We're dead serious about this project, Mr. Parker. I'd
like you to look at this chart.

THEO
And you'll see, we're not fooling. (*Hurriedly pins charts
taken from* BLUE'*s valise on wall out in the shop.*)

MR. PARKER
(*Reading from center chart.*) The Harlem De-Colonization Association, with Future Perspective for Bedford

Stuyvesant. (*Turns to* BLUE.) All right, so you got an organization. What do you do? I've never heard of you.

BLUE

The only reason you've never heard of us is because we don't believe in picketing, demonstrating, rioting, and all that stuff. We always look like we're doing something that we ain't doing, but we are doing something—and in that way nobody gets hurt. Now you may think we're passive. To the contrary, we believe in direct action. We are doers, enterprisers, thinkers—and most of all, we're businessmen! Our aim is to drive Mr. You-Know-Who out of Harlem.

MR. PARKER

Who's this Mr. You-Know-Who?

THEO

Damn, Pop! The white man!

MR. PARKER

Oh, himmm!

BLUE

We like to use that name for our members in order to get away from the bad feelings we have whenever we use the word "white." We want our members to always be objective and in this way we shall move forward. Before we get through, there won't be a single Mr. You-Know-Who left in this part of town. We're going to capture the imag-

75

ination of the people of Harlem. And that's never been done before, you know.

MR. PARKER
Now, tell me how?

BLUE
(*Standing before the charts, pointing with his cane.*) You see this here. This is what we call a "brigade." And you see this yellow circle?

MR. PARKER
What's that for?

BLUE
My new and entertaining system for playing the numbers. You do play the numbers, Mr. Parker?

MR. PARKER
I do.

BLUE
You see, I have a lot of colors in this system and these colors are mixed up with a whole lot of numbers, and the idea is to catch the right number with the right color. The right number can be anything from one to a hundred, but in order to win, the color must always be black. The name

of this game is called "Black Heaven." It's the color part that gives everybody all the fun in playing this game of mine.

MR. PARKER
Anybody ever catch it?

BLUE
Sure, but not until every number and every color has paid itself off. The one thing you'll find out about my whole operation: you can't lose. (*Pause for effect.*)

MR. PARKER
Keep talking.

BLUE
Now over here is the Red Square Circle Brigade, and this thing here is at the heart of my dream to create here in Harlem a symbolic life-force in the heart of the people.

MR. PARKER
You don't say . . .

BLUE
Put up that target, Theo. (THEO *hurriedly pins on wall a dart target with the face of a beefy, Southern-looking white man as bull's-eye.*)

77

MR. PARKER

Why, that's that ol' dirty sheriff from that little town in Mississippi!

BLUE

(*Taking a dart from* THEO.) That's right—we got a face on a target for every need. We got governors, mayors, backwood crackers, city crackers, Southern crackers, and Northern crackers. We got all kinds of faces on these targets that any good Harlemite would be willing to buy for the sake of slinging one of these darts in that bastard's throat! (*Throws dart, puncturing face on board.*)

MR. PARKER

Let me try it one time. (*Rising, takes dart from* BLUE *and slings it into the face on the target.*) Got him! (*A big laugh.*)

BLUE

It's like I said, Mr. Parker: the idea is to capture the imagination of the people!

MR. PARKER

You got more? Let me see more!

BLUE

Now this is our green circle—that's Theo and his corn liquor—for retail purposes will be called "Black Lightning." This whiskey of Theo's can make an everlasting contribution to this life-force I've been telling you about. I've tested this whiskey out in every neighborhood in Harlem, and everybody claimed it was the best they ever tasted this side of Washington, D.C. You see, we plan to supply every after-hours joint in this area, and this will run Mr. You-Know-Who and his bonded product out of Harlem.

THEO

You see, Pop, this all depends on the barbershop being open night and day so the people can come and go as they please, to pick up their play for the day, to get a bottle of corn, and to take one of them targets home to the kiddies. They can walk in just as if they were getting a haircut. In fact, I told Blue that we can give a haircut as a bonus for anyone who buys two quarts.

MR. PARKER

What am I suppose to say now?

THEO

You're suppose to be daring. You're suppose to wake up to the times, Pop! These are urgent days—a man has to stand up and be counted!

MR. PARKER

The police might have some counting of their own to do.

THEO

Do you think I would bring you into something that was

79

going to get us in trouble? Blue has an organization! Just like Mr. You-Know-Who. He's got members on the police force! In the city government, the state government.

BLUE

Mr. Parker, if you have any reservations concerning the operation of my association, I'd be only too happy to have you come to my summer home, and I'll let you in on every-thing—especially our protective system against being caught doing this thing.

THEO

Did you hear him, Pop, *he's got a summer home!*

MR. PARKER

Aw, shut up, boy! Let me think! (*Turns to* BLUE.) So you want to use my place as a headquarters for Theo's corn, the colored numbers, and them targets?

BLUE

Servicing the area of 125th to 145th, between the East and West rivers.

MR. PARKER

(*Pause.*)
I'm sorry, fellows, but I can't do it. (*Moves into back room.*)

THEO

(*Following* MR. PARKER.) Why?

MR. PARKER

It's not right.

THEO

Not right! What are you talking about? Is it right that all that's out there for us is to go downtown and push one of them carts? I have done that, and I ain't gon' do it no more!

MR. PARKER

That still don't make it right.

THEO

I don't buy it! I'm going into this thing with Blue, with or without you!

MR. PARKER

Go on, I don't care! You quit school, I couldn't stop you! I asked you to get a job, you wouldn't work! You have never paid any attention to any of my advice, and I don't expect you to start heeding me now!

THEO

Remember what you said to me about them paintings, and being what I am—well, this is me! At last I've found

81

what I can do, and it'll work—I know it will. Please, Pop, just—

MR. PARKER

Stop begging, Theo. (*Crosses back into shop, looks at* BLUE.) Why?

BLUE

I don't get you.

MR. PARKER

What kind of boy are you that you went through so much pain to dream up this cockeyed, ridiculous plan of yours?

BLUE

Mr. Parker, I was born about six blocks from here, and before I was ten I had the feeling I had been living for a hundred years. I got so old and tired I didn't know how to cry. Now you just think about that. But now I own a piece of this neighborhood. I don't have to worry about some bastard landlord or those credit crooks on 125th Street. Beautiful, black Blue—they have to worry about me! (*Reaches into his pocket and pulls out a stack of bills. Places them in* PARKER's *hands.*) Can't you see, man —I'm here to put you in business! (MR. PARKER *runs his fingers through the money.*) Money, Mr. Parker—brand-new money . . .

(After concentrated attention, MR. PARKER *drops money on table and moves into back room.* THEO *hurriedly follows.* MR. PARKER *sits on bed, in deep thought.)*

THEO

That's just to get us started. And if we can make a dent into Mr. You-Know-Who's going-ons in Harlem, nobody's going to think of us as crooks. We'll be heroes from 110th Street to Sugar Hill. And just think, Pop, you won't have to worry about jobs and all that. You'll have so much time for you and Mr. Jenkins to play checkers, your arms will drop off. You'll be able to sit as long as you want, and tell enough stories and lies to fit between the cover of a 500-page book. That's right! Remember you said you wanted to write all them stories down! Now you'll have time for it! You can dress up the way you used to. And the girls—remember how you used to be so tough with the girls before you got married? All that can come back to you, and some of that you never had. It's so easy! All you have to do is call Adele down those stairs and let her know that you're going into business and if she don't like it she can pack up and move out, because you're not going to let her drive you down because you're a man, and—

MR. PARKER

All right! *(Moves back into shop, where* BLUE *is putting away his paraphernalia.)* I'll do it!

(*Pause.*)

I'll do it under one condition—

BLUE
And that is?

MR. PARKER
If my buddy Jenkins wants to buy into this deal, you'll let him.

BLUE
Theo?

THEO
It's all right.

MR. PARKER
(*Extending his hand to* BLUE.) Then you got yourself some partners, Mr. Haven!

BLUE
Welcome into the association, Mr. Parker.

MR. PARKER
Welcome into my barbershop!

THEO
(*Jubilantly.*) Yehhhhhhhhhh!

(BLUE *checks his watch.* ADELE *comes into the back room.*)

BLUE

Well, I have to check out now, but I'll stop over tomorrow and we will set the whole thing up just as you want it, Mr. Parker. See you later, Theo.

MR. PARKER

(*To* BLUE *as he is walking out the front door.*) You should stick around awhile and watch my polish!

THEO

Pop, don't you think it would be better if you would let me give the word to Adele?

MR. PARKER

No. If I'm going to run a crooked house, *I'm* going to run it, and that goes for you as well as her.

THEO

But, Pop, sometimes she kinda gets by you.

MR. PARKER

Boy, I have never done anything like this in my life, but since I've made up my mind to it, you have nothing to say —not a word. You have been moaning about me never making it so you can have a chance. Well, this time you can say I'm with you. But let me tell you something: I don't want no more lies from you, and no more conning me about painting, airplane piloting, or nothing. If being a crook is what you want to be, you're going to be the best crook in the world—even if you have to drink mud to prove it.

THEO

(*Pause.*)
Okay, Pop.

MR. PARKER

(*Moves toward back room.*) Well, here goes nothing. Adele! (*Just as he calls,* ADELE *steps out of the back room, stopping him in his tracks.*)

ADELE

Yes, Father.

MR. PARKER

Oh, you're here already. Well, I want to talk to—well, I, er—

ADELE

What is it?

MR. PARKER

(*Pause.*)
Nothing. I'll talk to you later. (*He spots* BOBBY *entering from the outside with a package wrapped in newspaper.*) What you got there?

BOBBY

Uh . . . uh . . . —fish!

MR. PARKER

Well, you better get them in the refrigerator before they stink on you.

THEO

(*Going over to* BOBBY *and taking package from him.*) No, no. Now, Bobby, I promised Pop we would never lie to him again. It ain't fish, Pop. We've got something for you. (*Puts the package on the table and starts unwrapping it. The two boys stand over the table, and as the typewriter is revealed, both turn to him.*)

THEO and BOBBY

Happy Birthday!

MR. PARKER

Birthday? Birthday?

THEO and BOBBY

Yes, Happy Birthday!

MR. PARKER

Now hold on just a minute!

BOBBY

What are we holding on for, Pop?

MR. PARKER

(*Pause.*)

That's a good question, son. We're—we're holding on for a celebration! (*Laughs loudly.*) Thanks, fellows! But what am I going to do with a typewriter! I don't know nothing about no typing!

ADELE

I would like to know where they got the money to buy one!

THEO

(*Ignoring her.*) You know what you told me about writing down your stories—now you can write them down three times as fast!

MR. PARKER

But I don't know how to type!

THEO

With the money we're gonna be having, I can hire somebody to teach you!

ADELE

What money you going to have?

THEO

We're going into business, baby—right here in this barbershop!

MR. PARKER
Theo—

THEO
(*Paying no attention.*) We're going to sell bootleg whiskey, numbers, and—

ADELE
You're what!?

MR. PARKER
Theo—

THEO
You heard me, and if you don't like it you can pack your bags and leave!

ADELE
Leave? I pay the rent here!

THEO
No more! I pay it now!

MR. PARKER
Shut up, Theo!

THEO
We're going to show you something, girl. You think—

MR. PARKER
I said shut up!

ADELE
Is he telling the truth?

MR. PARKER
Yes, he is telling the truth.

ADELE
You mean to tell me you're going to turn this shop into a bootleg joint?

MR. PARKER
I'll turn it into anything I want to!

ADELE
Not while I'm still here!

MR. PARKER
The lease on this house has my signature, not yours!

ADELE
I'm not going to let you do this!

MR. PARKER
You got no choice, Adele. *You don't have a damn thing to say!*

90

ADELE

(*Turns sharply to* THEO.) You put him up to this!

MR. PARKER

Nobody puts me up to anything I don't want to do! These two boys have made it up in their minds they're not going to work for nobody but themselves, and the thought in my mind is *why should they!* I did like you said, I went downtown, and it's been a long time since I did that, but *you're* down there every day, and you oughta know by now that I am too old a man to ever dream I . . . could overcome the dirt and filth they got waiting for me down there. I'm surprised at you, that you would have so little care in you to shove me into the middle of that mob.

ADELE

You can talk about caring? What about Mama? She *died* working for you! Did you ever stop to think about that! In fact, *did you ever love her?* No!!!

MR. PARKER

That's a lie!

ADELE

I hope that one day you'll be able to do one good thing to drive that doubt out of my mind. *But this is not it!* You've let this hoodlum sell you his twisted ideas of making a short cut through life. But let me tell you something— this bastard is going to ruin you!

THEO

(*Into her face.*) Start packing, baby!

ADELE

(*Strikes him across the face.*) Don't you talk to me like
that!

(*He raises his hand to strike her back.*)

MR. PARKER

Drop your hand, boy! (THEO *does not respond.*) I said,
drop your goddamn hand!

THEO

She hit me!

MR. PARKER

I don't care if she had broken your jaw. If you ever draw
your hand back to hit this girl again—*as long as you* live!
You better not be in my hand reach when you do, 'cause
I'll split your back in two! (*To* ADELE.) We're going into
business, Adele. I have come to that and I have come to
it on my own. I am going to stop worrying once and for
all whether I live naked in the cold or whether I die like
an animal, unless I can live the best way I know how to.
I am getting old and I oughta have some fun. I'm going to
get me some money, and I'm going to spend it! I'm going
to get drunk! I'm going to dance some more! *I'm getting
old! I'm going to fall in love one more time before I die!*

So get to that, girl, and if it's too much for you to bear, I wouldn't hold it against you if you walked away from here this very minute—

ADELE

(*Opens the door to the back room to show him the birthday surprise she has for him.*) Happy birthday!

MR. PARKER

(*Goes into the room and stands over table where birthday cake is.*) I guess I fooled all of you. Today is not my birthday. It never was. (*Moves up the stairs.*)

ADELE

It's not going to work! You're going to cut your throat— you hear me! You're going to rip yourself into little pieces! (*Turns to* THEO.) It's not going to be the way you want it—because I know Mr. Blue Haven, and he is not a person to put your trust in. (THEO *turns his back on her, heads for the shop door.*) . . . I am talking to you!

THEO

(*Stops and turns.*) Why don't you leave us alone. You're the one who said we had to go out and do something. Well, we did, but we're doing it our way. Me and Bobby, we're men—if we lived the way you wanted us to, we wouldn't have nothing but big fat veins popping out of our heads.

ADELE

I'll see what kind of men you are every time a cop walks
through that door, every time a stranger steps into this
back room and you can't be too sure about him, and the
day they drag your own father off and throw him into a
jail cell.

THEO

But, tell me, what else is there left for us to do. You tell
me and I'll do it. You show me where I can go to spin the
world around before it gets too late for somebody like
Mama living fifty years just to die on 126th Street! *You
tell me of a place where there are no old crippled vaudeville men!*

ADELE

There is no such place.

(*Pause.*)

But you don't get so hung up about it you have to plunge
a knife into your own body. You don't bury yourself here
in this place; you climb up out of it! Now that's something
for you to wonder about, boy.

THEO

I wonder all the time—how you have lived here all your
whole life on this street, and you haven't seen, heard,

learned, or felt a thing in all those years. I wonder how you ever got to be such a damn fool!

CURTAIN

ACT TWO

SCENE ONE

———◆———

Two months later. It is about 9 P.M.

As the curtain rises, the lights come up in the back room.
BOBBY *is there, listening to a record of James Brown's*
"Money Won't Change You, But Time Will Take You On."
As he is dancing out to the shop, THEO *appears from the cel-*
lar, which has been enlarged by taking out a panel in the
lower section of the wall and houses the whiskey-making
operation. THEO *brings in two boxes filled with bottles of*
corn whiskey and shoves them under the bed.

BOBBY *moves past* THEO *into the shop, carrying a target*
rolled up in his hand, and two darts. He is wearing a fancy
sports shirt, new trousers, new keen-toed shoes, and a stingy,
diddy-bop hat. He pins the target up on the wall of the shop.
In the center of the target is the face of a well-known Amer-
ican racist.

BOBBY

(*Moves away from the target, aims and hurls the dart.*)
That's for Pop! Huh! (*Throws another.*) And this is for
me! Huh! (*Moves to the target to pull darts out.* THEO
cuts record off abruptly. A knock at the door.)

THEO

(*Calling out to* BOBBY *from the back room.*) Lock that
door!

BOBBY

Lock it yourself!

THEO

(*With quick but measured steps moves toward front
door.*) I'm not selling another bottle, target, or anything,
till I get some help! (*Locks door in spite of persistent
knocking.*) We're closed!

BOBBY

I don't think Blue is gon' like you turning customers away.
(*Sits in barber chair, lighting up cigar.*)

THEO

You can tell Blue I don't like standing over that stove all
day, that I don't like him promising me helpers that don't
show up. There are a lot of things I don't go for, like Pop
taking off and not showing up for two days. I make this
whiskey, I sell it, I keep books, I peddle numbers and

those damn targets. *And I don't like you standing around here all day not lifting a finger to help me!*

BOBBY

(*Taking a big puff on his cigar.*) I don't hear you.

THEO

Look at you—all decked out in your new togs. Look at me: I haven't been out of these dungarees since we opened this place up.

BOBBY

(*Jumps out of chair.*) I don't wanta hear nothing! You do what you wanta do, and leave me alone!

THEO

What am I supposed to be, a work mule or something?

BOBBY

You're the one that's so smart—you can't answer your own stupid questions?

THEO

You done let Blue turn you against me, huh?

BOBBY

You ask the questions, and you gon' answer them—but for now, stop blowing your breath in my face!

THEO

You make me sick. (*Moves into back room. Sits on bed.*)

ADELE

(*Enters from upstairs, dressed in a smart Saks Fifth Avenue outfit.*) Getting tired already, Theo?

THEO

No, just once in a while I'd like to have some time to see one of my women!

ADELE

You being the big industrialist and all that, I thought you had put girls off for a year or two!

THEO

Get away from me. (*Crosses to desk and sits.*)

ADELE

I must say, however—it is sure a good sight to see you so wrapped up in work. I never thought I'd live to see the day, but—

THEO

Don't you ever have anything good to say?

ADELE

I say what I think and feel. I'm honest

THEO

Honest? You're just hot because Pop decided to do something my way for a change.

ADELE

That's a joke, when you haven't seen him for two whole days. Or, *do* you know where he has gone to practically every night since you opened up this little store.

THEO

He's out having a little sport for himself. What's wrong with that? He hasn't had any fun in a long time.

ADELE

Is fun all you can think of? When *my* father doesn't show up for two days, I worry.

THEO

You're not worried about nobody but yourself—I'm on to your game. You'd give anything in the world to go back just the way we were, because you liked the idea of us being dependent on you. Well, that's all done with, baby. We're on our own. So don't worry yourself about Pop. When Blue gets here tonight with our money, he'll be here!

ADELE

If my eyes and ears are clear, then I would say that Father

isn't having the kind of money troubles these days that he must rush home for your pay day.

THEO

What do you mean by that?

ADELE

I mean that he has been dipping his hands into that little drawer of yours at least two or three times a week.

THEO

You ain't telling nothing I don't know.

ADELE

What about your friend Blue?

THEO

I can handle him.

ADELE

I hope so, since it is a known fact that he can be pretty evil when he thinks someone has done him wrong—and it happened once, in a bar uptown, he actually killed a man.

THEO

You're lying. (*He moves quickly to shop entrance.*) Bobby, have you heard anything about Blue killing a man? (BOBBY, *seated in the barber's chair, looks at him, then turns away, not answering.* THEO *returns to the back room.*)

ADELE

Asking him about it is not going to help you. Ask yourself a few questions and you will know that you are no better than Blue—because it is you two who are the leaders of those mysterious store raids on 125th Street, and your ace boy on those robberies is no one other than your brother, Bobby Parker!

THEO

Bobby!

ADELE

I don't know why that should surprise you, since he is known as the swiftest and coolest young thief in Harlem.

THEO

I didn't know about Bobby—*who told you!*

ADELE

As you well know by now, I've been getting around lately, and I meet people, and people like to have something to talk about, and you know something: this place is becoming the talk along every corner and bar on the Avenue!

THEO

You're just trying to scare me.

ADELE

I wish to God I was. (*Starts out.*)

THEO

Where are you going?

ADELE

(*Stops, turns abruptly.*) Out. Do you mind?

THEO

That's all you ever do!

ADELE

Yes, you're right.

THEO

They tell me you're going with Wilmer Robinson?

ADELE

Yes, that's true. (*Moving through shop toward door.* BOBBY *doesn't move from the barber's throne and buries his nose in a comic book.*)

THEO

(*Following behind her.*) He's a snake.

ADELE

No better or worse than someone like you or Blue.

THEO

He'll bleed you for every dime you've got!

ADELE

So what. He treats me like a woman, and that's more than
I can say for any man in this house!

THEO

He'll treat you like a woman until he's gotten everything
he wants, and then he's gon' split your ass wide open!

ADELE

(*Turns sharply at door.*) Theooooooooooo!

(*Pause.*)

You talk like that to me because you don't know how to
care for the fact that I am your sister.

THEO

But why are you trying to break us up? Why?

ADELE

I don't have to waste that kind of good time. I can wait
for you to bust it up yourself. Good night! (*Slams the door
behind herself.*)

(THEO *stands with a long, deep look in his eyes, then goes
down cellar.* MR. PARKER *steps into the shop, all dapper,*

dressed up to a fare-thee-well, holding a gold-top cane in one hand and a book in the other. BOBBY *stares at him, bewildered.*)

BOBBY

What's that you got on?

MR. PARKER

What does it look like?

BOBBY

Nothing.

MR. PARKER

You call this nothing!

BOBBY

Nothing—I mean, I didn't mean nothing when I asked you that question.

MR. PARKER

Where's Theo?

BOBBY

In the back, working.

MR. PARKER

Good! Shows he's got his mind stretched out for good and great things. (*Hangs up hat and puts away cane.*)

BOBBY

He's been stretching his mind out to find out where you
been.

MR. PARKER

Where I been is none of his business, Blue is the man to
think about. It's pay day, and I wanta know, where the
hell is he! (*Checks his watch, taps* BOBBY, *indicating he
should step down from chair.*)

BOBBY

(*Hops down from chair.* PARKER *sits.*) Whatcha reading?

MR. PARKER

A book I picked up yesterday. I figured since I'm in business I might as well read a businessman's book.

BOBBY

Let me see it. (*Takes the book in his hand.*) *The Thief's
Journal*, by Jean Gin-nett. (*Fingering through pages.*) Is
it a good story?

MR. PARKER

So far—

BOBBY

(*Hands it back.*) What's it all about?

MR. PARKER

A Frenchman who was a thief.

BOBBY

Steal things?

MR. PARKER

Uh-huh.

BOBBY

Where did he get all that time to write a book?

MR. PARKER

Oh, he had the time all right, 'cause he spent most of it in jail.

BOBBY

Some thief!

MR. PARKER

The trouble with this bird is that he became a thief and then he became a thinker.

BOBBY

No shucking!

MR. PARKER

No shucking. But it is my logicalism that you've got to become a thinker and then you become a crook! Or else,

why is it when you read up on some of these politicians'
backgrounds you find they all went to one of them big
law colleges? That's where you get your start!

BOBBY

Well, I be damned!

MR. PARKER

(*Jumps down out of the chair, moves briskly toward
door.*) Now where is Blue! He said he would be here nine-
thirty on the nose! (*Opens the door and* JENKINS *comes
in.*) Hey, Jenkins! What's up!

MR. JENKINS

That Blue fellow show up yet?

MR. PARKER

No, he didn't, and I'm gon' call him down about that too.

MR. JENKINS

It don't matter. I just want whatever money I got coming,
and then I'm getting out of this racket.

MR. PARKER

Don't call it that, it's a committee!

MR. JENKINS

This committee ain't no committee. It ain't nothing but a
racket, and I'm getting out of it!

MR. PARKER

You put your money into this thing, man. It ain't good business to walk out on an investment like that.

MR. JENKINS

I can, and that's what I'm doing before I find myself in jail! Man, this thing you got going here is the talk in every bar in this neighborhood.

MR. PARKER

There ain't nothing for you to be scared of, Jenkins. Blue guaranteed me against ever being caught by the police. Now that's all right by me, but I've got some plans of my own. When he gets here tonight, I'm gon' force him to make me one of the leaders in this group, and if he don't watch out, I just might take the whole operation over from him. I'll make you my right-hand man, and not only will you be getting more money, and I won't just guarantee you against getting caught, but I'll guarantee you against being scared!

MR. JENKINS

There's nothing you can say to make me change my mind. I shouldn't've let you talk me into this mess in the first place. I'm getting out, and that's it! (*Starts for the door.*) And if he gets back before I do, you hold my money for me! (*Exiting.*)

MR. PARKER

(*Pursuing him to door.*) Suit yourself, but you're cutting
your own throat. This little set-up is the biggest thing to
hit this neighborhood since the day I started dancing!
(*Slams door.*) Fool! (*Takes off coat, hangs it up. Goes
to mirror to primp.*)

BOBBY

Going somewhere again?

MR. PARKER

Got myself a little date to get to if Blue ever gets here with
our money—*and he better get here with our money!*

BOBBY

You been dating a lot lately—nighttime dates, and day
ones too—and Theo's not happy about it. He says you
don't stay here long enough to cut Yul Brynner's hair.

MR. PARKER

He can complain all he wants to. I'm the boss here, and
he better not forget it. He's the one that's got some ex-
plaining to do: don't talk to nobody no more, don't go
nowhere, looking like he's mad all the time . . . I've
also noticed that he don't get along with you any more.

BOBBY

Well, Pop, that's another story.

MR. PARKER

Come on, boy, there's something on his mind, and you know what it is.

BOBBY

(*Moving away.*) Nothing, except he wants to tell me what to do all the time. But I've got some ideas of my own. I ain't no dumbbell; I just don't talk as much as he do. If I did, the people I talk to would know just as much as I do. I just want him to go his way, and I'll go mine.

MR. PARKER

There's more to it than that, and I wanta know what it is.

BOBBY

There's nothing.

MR. PARKER

Come on now, boy.

BOBBY

That's all, Pop!

MR. PARKER

(*Grabs him.*) It's not, and you better say something!

BOBBY

He—I don't know what to tell you, Pop. He just don't like the way things are going—with you, me—Adele. He got in a fight with her today and she told him about Blue killing a man.

MR. PARKER

Is it true?

BOBBY

Yeah. Blue killed this man one time for saying something about his woman, and this woman got a child by Blue but Blue never married her and so this man started signifying about it. Blue hit him, the man reached for a gun in his pocket, Blue took the gun from him, and the—man started running, but by that time Blue had fire in his eyes, and he shot the man three times.

MR. PARKER

Well . . .

BOBBY

Blue got only two years for it!

MR. PARKER

Two years, hunh? That's another thing I'm gon' throw in his face tonight if he tries to get smart with me. Ain't that something. Going around bumping people off, and getting away with it too! What do he think he is, white or something! (THEO *comes in and sits at desk.* MR. PARKER *checks his watch.*) I'm getting tired of this! (*Moves into back room.*) Where's that friend of yours!? I don't have to wait around this barbershop all night for him. It's been two months now, and I want my money! When I say be here at nine-thirty, I mean be here!

THEO

(*Rising from desk.*) Where have you been, Pop?

MR. PARKER

That's none of your business! Now where is that man with my money!

THEO

Money is not your problem—you've been spending it all over town! And you've been taking it out of this desk!

MR. PARKER

So? I borrowed a little.

THEO

You call four hundred dollars a little! Now I've tried to fix these books so it don't show too big, and you better hope Blue don't notice it when he starts fingering through these pages tonight.

MR. PARKER

To hell with Blue! It's been two months now, and he ain't shown us a dime!

THEO

What are you doing with all that money, Pop?

MR. PARKER

I don't have to answer to you! I'm the boss here. And another thing, there's a lot about Blue and this association I want to know about. I want a position! I don't have to sit around here every month or so, waiting for somebody to bring me *my* money.

THEO

Money! Money! That's all you can think about!

MR. PARKER

Well, look who's talking. You forget this was all your idea. Remember what I told you about starting something and sticking with it. What is it now, boy? The next thing you'll tell me is that you've decided to become a priest or something. What's the new plan, Theo?

THEO

No new plans, Pop. I just don't want us to mess up. Don't you understand—things must be done right, or else we're going to get ourselves in jail. We have to be careful, we have to think about each other all the time. I didn't go into this business just for myself, I wasn't out to prove how wrong Adele was. I just thought the time had come for us to do something about all them years we laid around here letting Mama kill herself!

MR. PARKER

I have told you a thousand times I don't wanta hear any talk about your mama. She's dead, damnit! So let it stay that way! (*Moves toward shop.*)

THEO

All right, let's talk about Adele then.

MR. PARKER

(*Stopping at steps.*) What about her?

THEO

She's out of this house every night.

MR. PARKER

Boy, you surprise me. What do you think she should do, work like a dog all day and then come to this house and bite her fingernails all night?

THEO

She's got herself a boy friend too, and—

MR. PARKER

(*Crossing to counter.*) Good! I got myself a girl friend, now that makes two of us!

THEO

(*Following him.*) But he's—aw, what's the use. But I wish you'd stay in the shop more!

MR. PARKER

That's too bad. I have things to do. I don't worry about where you're going when you leave here.

THEO

I don't go anywhere and you know it. If I did, we wouldn't do an hour's business. *But we have been doing great business!* And you wanta know why? They love it! *Everybody* loves the way ol' Theo brews corn! Every after-hours joint is burning with it! And for us to do that kind of business, I've had to sweat myself down in this hole for something like sixteen hours a day for two whole months!

MR. PARKER

What do you want from me?

THEO

I just want you here in the shop with me, so at least we can pretend that this is a barbershop. A cop walked through that door today while I had three customers in here, and I had to put one of them in that chair and cut his hair!

MR. PARKER

How did you make out?

THEO

Pop, I don't need your jokes!

MR. PARKER

All right, don't get carried away. (*Goes to* THEO *and puts his arm around the boy's shoulders.*) I'll make it my business to stay here in the shop with you more.

THEO

And make Blue guarantee me some help.

MR. PARKER

You'll get that too. But you've got to admit one thing, though—you've always been a lazy boy. I didn't expect you to jump and all of a sudden act like John Henry!

THEO

I have never been lazy. I just didn't wanta break my back for the man!

MR. PARKER

Well, I can't blame you for that. I know, because I did it. I did it when they didn't pay me a single dime!

BOBBY

When was that?

MR. PARKER

When I was on the chain gang!

BOBBY

Now you know you ain't never been on no chain gang!

MR. PARKER

(*Holds up two fingers.*) Two months, that's all it was.
Just two months.

BOBBY

Two months, my foot!

MR. PARKER

I swear to heaven I was. It was in 19-something, I was
living in Jersey City, New Jersey . . . (*Crosses to throne
and sits.*)

BOBBY

Here we go with another story!

MR. PARKER

That was just before I started working as a vaudeville
man, and there was this ol' cousin of mine we used to
call "Dub," and he had this job driving a trailer truck
from Jersey City to Jacksonville, Florida. One day he
asked me to come along with him for company. I weren't
doing nothing at the time, and—

BOBBY

As usual.

MR. PARKER

I didn't say that! Anyway, we drove along. Everything
was fine till we hit Macon, Georgia. We weren't doing a

121

thing, but before we knew it this cracker police stopped us, claiming we'd ran through a red light. He was yelling and hollering and, boyyy, did I get mad—I was ready to get a hold of that cracker and work on his head until . . .

BOBBY

Until what?

MR. PARKER

Until they put us on the chain gang, and the chain gang they put us on was a chain gang and a half! I busted some rocks John Wayne couldn't've busted! I was a rock-busting fool! (*Rises and demonstrates how he swung the hammer.*) I would do it like this! I would hit the rock, and the hammer would bounce—bounce so hard it would take my hand up in the air with it—but I'd grab it with my left hand and bring it down like this: Hunh! (*Carried away by the rhythm of his story, he starts twisting his body to the swing of it.*) It would get so good to me, I'd say: Hunh! Yeah! Hunh! I'd say, Oooooooooooweeeee! I'm wide open now! (*Swinging and twisting.*) Yeah, baby, I say, Hunh! Sooner or later that rock would crack! Old Dub ran into a rock one day that was hard as Theo's head. He couldn't bust that rock for nothing. He pumped and swung, but that rock would not move. So finally he said to the captain: "I'm sorry, Cap, but a elephant couldn't break this rock." Cap didn't wanna hear nothing. He said, "Well, Dub, I wanna tell you something—your lunch and your supper is in the middle of that rock." On the next swing of the hammer, Dub busted that rock into a thousand pieces! (*Laughs.*) I'm telling you, them crackers is mean. Don't let nobody tell you about no Communists, Chinese, or anything: there ain't nothing on this earth meaner and dirtier than an American-born cracker! We used to sleep in them long squad tents on the ground, and we was all hooked up to this one big long chain: the guards had orders to shoot at random in the dark if ever one of them chains would rattle. You couldn't even turn over in your sleep! (*Sits on throne.*)

BOBBY

A man can't help but turn over in his sleep!

MR. PARKER

Not on this chain gang you didn't. You turn over on this chain gang in your sleep and your behind was shot! But if you had to, you would have to wake up, announce that you was turning over, and then you go back to sleep!

BOBBY

What!

MR. PARKER

Just like this. (*Illustrating physically.*) "Number 4 turning over!" But that made all the chains on the other convicts rattle, so they had to turn over too and shout: "Number 5 turning over! Number 6 turning over! Number 7!"

THEO

Why don't you stop it!

MR. PARKER

I ain't lying!

BOBBY

Is that all?

MR. PARKER

Yeah, and I'm gon' get Adele to type that up on my type-writer! (*Goes to the window.*) Now where the hell is that Blue Haven!

MR. JENKINS

(*Rushing in.*) Did he show up yet?

MR. PARKER

Naw, and when he does, I'm—

MR. JENKINS

I told you I didn't trust that boy—who knows where he is! Well, I'm going out there and get him! (*Starts back out.*)

MR. PARKER

(*Grabs him by the arm.*) Now don't go out there messing with Blue, Jenkins! If there's anybody got a reason for being mad with him, it's me. Now take it easy. When he gets here, we'll all straighten him out. Come on, sit down and let me beat you a game one time. (*Takes board out quickly.*)

BOBBY

Tear him up, Pop!

MR. JENKINS

(*Pause.*)

Okay, you're on. (*Moves toward* MR. PARKER *and the table.*) It's hopeless. I been playing your father for three solid years, and he has yet to beat me one game!

MR. PARKER

Yeah! But his luck done come to past!

MR. JENKINS

My luck ain't come to past, 'cause my luck is skill. (*Spelling the word out.*) S-K-I-L-L.

MR. PARKER

(*Shakes up the can.*) Come on now, Jenkins, let's play the game. Take one. (MR. JENKINS *pulls out a checker.*) You see there, you get the first move.

MR. JENKINS

You take me for a fool, Parker, and just for that I ain't gon' let you get a king.

MR. PARKER

Put your money where your lips is. I say I'm gon' win this
game!

MR. JENKINS

I don't want your money, I'm just gon' beat you!

MR. PARKER

I got twenty dollars here to make a liar out of you! (*Slams
down a twenty-dollar bill on the table.*) Now you doing
all the bragging about how I never beat you, but I'm
valiant enough to say that, from here on in, you can't win
air, and I got twenty dollars up on the table to back it up.

MR. JENKINS

Oh, well, he ain't satisfied with me beating him all the
time for sport. He wants me to take his money too.

MR. PARKER

But that's the difference.

MR. JENKINS

What kind of difference?

MR. PARKER

We're playing for money, and I don't think you can play
under that kind of pressure. You do have twenty dollars,
don't you?

MR. JENKINS

I don't know what you're laughing about, I always keep some money on me. (*Pulls out change purse and puts twenty dollars on the table.*) You get a little money in your pocket and you get carried away.

MR. PARKER

It's your move.

MR. JENKINS

Start you off over here in this corner.

MR. PARKER

Give you that little ol' fellow there.

MR. JENKINS

I'll take him.

MR. PARKER

I'll take this one.

MR. JENKINS

I'll give you this man here.

MR. PARKER

I'll jump him—so that you can have this one

MR. JENKINS

I'll take him.

MR. PARKER

Give you this man here.

MR. JENKINS

All right. (*He moves.*)

MR. PARKER

I'll take this one. (*Series of grunts and groans as they exchange men.*) And I'll take these three. (*Jumping* MR. JENKINS's *men and laughing loud.*) Boom! Boom! Boom! (*The game is now definitely in favor of* MR. PARKER. MR. JENKINS *is pondering over his situation. Relishing* MR. JENKINS's *predicament:*) Study long, you study wrong. I'm afraid that's you, ol' buddy . . . I knew it, I knew it all the time—I used to ask myself: I wonder how ol' Jenks would play if he really had some pressure on him? You remember how the Dodgers used to raise hell every year until they met the Yankees in the World Series, and how under all that pressure they would crack up? (*Laughs.*) That pressure got him!

MR. JENKINS

Hush up, man. I'm trying to think!

MR. PARKER

I don't know what you could be thinking about, 'cause the rooster done came and wrote, skiddy biddy!

128

MR. JENKINS

(*Finally makes a move.*) There!

MR. PARKER

(*In sing-song.*) That's all—that's all . . . (*Makes another jump.*) Boom! Just like you say, Bobby—"tear him up!" (*Rears his head back in ecstatic laughter.*)

MR. JENKINS

(*Makes a move.*) It's your move.

MR. PARKER

(*His laughter trails off sickly as he realizes that the game is now going his opponent's way.*) Well, I see. I guess that kinda changes the color of the game . . . Let me see now . . .

MR. JENKINS

(*Getting his revenge.*) Why don't you laugh some more? I like the way you laugh, Parker.

MR. PARKER

Shut up, Jenkins. I'm thinking!

MR. JENKINS

Thinking? Thinking for what? The game is over! (*Now he is laughing hard.* MR. PARKER *ruefully makes his move.*) Uh-uh! Lights out! (*Still laughing, answers* PARK·

ER's *move*.) Game time, and you know it! Take your jump! (MR. PARKER *is forced to take his jump*. JENKINS *takes his opponent's last three men*.) I told you about laughing and bragging in my game! Boom! Boom! Boom!

MR. PARKER

(*Rises abruptly from the table and dashes to coat rack*.) DAMNIT!!!

MR. JENKINS

Where you going—ain't we gon' play some more?

MR. PARKER

(*Putting on coat*.) I don't wanta play you no more. You too damn lucky!

MR. JENKINS

Aw, come on, Parker. I don't want your money, I just want to play!

MR. PARKER

You won it, you keep it—I can *afford* it! But one of these days you're going to leave that voodoo root of yours home, and that's gonna be the day—you hear me, you sonofabitch!

BOBBY

Pop!

MR. PARKER

I don't want to hear nothing from you!

MR. JENKINS

(*Realizing that* PARKER *is really upset.*) It's only a game
—and it don't have nothing to do with luck . . . But
you keep trying, Parker, and one of these days you're
going to beat me. And when you do, it won't have nothing
to do with luck—it just might be the unluckiest and worst
day of your life. You'll be champion checker player of the
world. Meanwhile, I'm the champ, *and you're gonna have
to live with it.*

MR. PARKER

(*Smiling, grudgingly moves toward him with his hand
extended.*) All right, Jenkins! You win this time, but I'm
gon' beat you yet. I'm gon' whip your behind until it turns
white!

BOBBY

That's gon' be some strong whipping! (*There's a tap at
the door.*) That must be Blue. (*Rushes to the door and
opens it.*)

MR. PARKER

About time. (BLUE *enters.*) Hey, boy, where have you
been?

131

BLUE

(*Moves in, carrying an attaché case.*) I got stuck with an emergency council meeting.

MR. PARKER

What kind of council?

BLUE

The council of the Association. I see you're sporting some new clothes there, Mr. P. You must be rolling in extra dough these days.

MR. PARKER

Just a little something I picked up the other day. All right, where is the money, Blue?

BLUE

You'll get your money, but first I want to see those books. (*Moves to the desk in the back room and starts going over the books. In the shop an uneasy silence prevails.* JENKINS, *out of nervousness, sets up the checkers for another game.*)

BLUE

I see. (*Takes out pencil and pad and starts scribbling on a sheet of paper.*) Uh-huh. Uh-huh . . . (*Re-enters shop.*)

132

MR. PARKER

Well?

BLUE

Everything seems to be okay.

MR. PARKER

Of course everything is all right. What did you expect? (*Angry, impatient.*) Now come on and give me my money.

BLUE

Take it easy, Mr. Parker! (*Takes a white envelope from his case and passes it on to* PARKER.) Here's your money.

MR. PARKER

Now this is what I like to see!

BLUE

(*Passes some bills to* MR. JENKINS.) And you, Mr. Jenkins.

MR. JENKINS

Thank you, young man. But from here on in, you can count me out of your operation.

BLUE

What's the trouble?

MR. JENKINS

No trouble at all. I just want to be out of it.

BLUE

People and headaches—that's all I ever get from all the Mr. Jenkinses in this world!

MR. JENKINS

Why don't you be quiet sometime, boy.

MR. PARKER

I'm afraid he's telling you right, Blue.

BLUE

He's telling me that he is a damn idiot, who can get himself hurt!

THEO

Who's going to hurt him?

(*They all stare at* BLUE.)

BLUE

(*Calming down.*) I'm sorry. I guess I'm working too hard these days. I got a call today from one of them "black committees" here in Harlem . . .

THEO

What did they want?

BLUE

They wanted to know what we did. They said they had heard of us, but they never see us—meaning they never see us picketing, demonstrating, and demanding something all the time.

MR. PARKER

So?

BLUE

They want us to demonstrate with them next Saturday, and I have decided to set up a demonstrating committee, with you in charge, Mr. Parker.

MR. PARKER

You what!

BLUE

You'd be looking good!

MR. PARKER

You hear that! (*Cynical laughter.*) *I'd be looking good!* Count me out! When I demonstrate, it's for real!

BLUE

You demonstrate in front of any store out there on that street, and you'll have a good sound reason for being there!

MR. PARKER

I thought you said we was suppose to be different, and we was to drive out that Mr. You-Know-Somebody—well, ain't that what we doing? Two stores already done put up "going out of business" signs.

BLUE

That's what we started this whole thing for, and that's what we're doing.

MR. PARKER

I got some questions about that, too. I don't see nothing that we're doing that would cause a liquor store, a clothing store, and a radio store to just all of a sudden close down like that, unless we've been raiding and looting them at night or something like that.

(BOBBY *quickly moves out of the shop into the back room and exits upstairs.*)

BLUE

It's the psychological thing that's doing it, man!

MR. PARKER

Psychological? Boy, you ain't telling me everything, and anyway I wanta know who made this decision about picketing.

BLUE

The council!

MR. PARKER

Who is on this council?

BLUE

You know we don't throw names around like that!

MR. PARKER

I don't get all the mystery, Blue. This is my house, and you know everything about it from top to bottom. I got my whole family in this racket!

BLUE

You're getting a good share of the money—ain't that enough?

MR. PARKER

Not when I'm dealing with you in the dark.

BLUE

You're asking for something, so stop beating around corners and tell me what it is you want!

MR. PARKER

All right! You been promising my boy some help for two months now, and he's still waiting. Now I want you to give him that help starting tomorrow, and I want you to put somebody in this shop who can cut hair to relieve me when I'm not here. And from here on in, I want to know everything that's to be known about this "de-colonization committee"—how it works, who's in it, who's running it —*and I want to be on that council you was talking about!*

BLUE

NO!

MR. PARKER

Then I can't cooperate with you any more!

BLUE

What does that mean?

MR. PARKER

It means we can call our little deal off, and you can take your junk out of here!

BLUE

Just like that?

MR. PARKER

Just any ol' way you want it. I take too many risks in this place, not to know where I stand.

BLUE

Mr. Parker—

MR. PARKER

All right, let me hear it and let me hear it quick!

BLUE

There is an opening on our council. It's a—

MR. PARKER

Just tell me what position is it!

BLUE

President.

MR. PARKER

President?

BLUE

The highest office on our council.

MR. PARKER

Boy, you're gonna have to get up real early to get by an old fox like me. A few minutes ago you offered me nothing, and now you say I can be president—that should even sound strange to *you!*

BLUE

There's nothing strange. A few minutes ago you weren't ready to throw me out of your place, but now *I've got no other choice!*

MR. PARKER

(*Pointing his finger at him and laughing.*) That's true! You don't! All right, I'll give you a break—I accept! Just let me know when the next meeting is. (*Checks watch and grabs his hat.*) Come on, Jenkins, let's get out of here! (*Starts out with* MR. JENKINS.)

THEO

Hey, Pop—you're going out there with all that money in your pocket.

MR. PARKER

Don't worry about it. I'm a grown man, I can take care of myself.

THEO

But what about our part of it?

MR. PARKER

Look, son, he held me up—I'm late already. You'll get yours when I get back.

THEO

But, Pop—

MR. PARKER

Good night, Theo! (*Bolts out the door, with* MR. JENKINS *following.*)

THEO

(*Rushes to the door.*) Pop, you better be careful! I'll be waiting for you! I don't care if it's till dawn!

BLUE

You're becoming a worrier, Theo!

(*Pause.*)

But that's the nature of all things . . . I'm forever soothing and pacifying someone. Sometimes I have to pacify myself. You don't think that president stuff is going to mean anything, do you? He had me up-tight, so what I did was to bring him closer to me so I would be definitely sure of letting him know less and having more control over him—and over you, too.

THEO

What do you mean by that?

BLUE

It didn't take me more than one glance into those books to know that he's been spending money out of the box. And to think—you didn't bother to tell me about it.

THEO

Why should I? I trust your intelligence.

BLUE

Please don't let him do it any more.

THEO

Why don't you hire your own cashier and bookkeeper? (*He goes into back room.*)

BLUE

(*Following him.*) That's an idea! What about Adele! Now that was a thought in the back of my mind, but I'm putting that away real quick. Seems this sweet, nice-girl sister of yours has took to partying with the good-time set and keeping company with a simple ass clown like Wilmer Robinson. No, that wouldn't work, would it? I'd have more trouble with her than I'm having with you. When a girl as intelligent as your sister, who all of a sudden gets into things, and hooked up to people who just don't go with her personality, that could mean trouble. To be honest with you, I didn't think this thing was going to work, but *it is working,* Theo! I've got three places just like this one, and another on the way. A man has to care about what he does. Don't you want to get out of this place?

THEO

Yes, but lately I've been getting the feeling that I'm gonna have to hurt someone.

BLUE

I see.

THEO

You think the old man was asking you those questions about stores closing down as a joke or something?

BLUE

He asks because he thinks, but he is still in the dark!

THEO

He was playing with you! And when my father holds something inside of him and plays with a man, he's getting meaner and more dangerous by the minute.

BLUE

I don't care what he was doing—he is messing with my work! He has gotten himself into a "thing" with one of the rottenest bitches on the Avenue, who happens to be tight with a nigger who is trying to fuck up my business. Now that's something you had better get straight: it's your turn to soothe and pacify!

THEO

Why should I do anything for you when you lied to me and sent my brother out with that band of thieves of yours?

143

BLUE

He said he needed the money, and I couldn't stop him.

THEO

But I told you I didn't want that!

BLUE

Let's face it, baby! Bobby's the greatest thief in the world! He's been prancing around stores and stealing all of his life! And I think that's something to bow down to—because he's black and in trouble, just like you and me. So don't ride me so hard, Theo! (*They cross back into shop. He picks up attaché case, preparing to leave.*)

THEO

Blue! Now I don't care what kind of protection you got, but I say those store raids are dangerous and I don't want my brother on them, and I mean it!

BLUE

When we first made our plans, you went along with it— you knew somebody had to do it. What makes you and your brother so special?

THEO

Well, you better—

BLUE

To hell with you, Theo! I could take this hand and make you dead! You are nothing but what I make you be!

THEO

(*Pause.*)

That just might be. But what if tomorrow this whole operation were to bust wide open in your face because of some goof-up by my father or sister—something that would be just too much for you to clean up. What would you do? Kill them?

BLUE

(*Pause. Then calmly and deliberately.*) The other day I went up on the hill to see my little boy. I took him out for a ride and as we were moving along the streets he asked me where all the people were coming from. I said from work, going home, going to the store, and coming back from the store. Then we went out to watch the river and then he asked me about the water, the ships, the weeds—everything. That kid threw so many questions at me, I got dizzy—I wanted to hit him once to shut him up. He was just a little dark boy discovering for the first time that there are things in the world like stones and trees . . . It got late and dark, so I took him home and watched him fall asleep. Then I took his mother into my arms and put her into bed. I just laid there for a while, listening to her call me all kinds of dirty mother-fuckers. After she got that out of her system, I put my hands on her and before long our arms were locked at each other's shoulders and then my thighs moved slowly down between her thighs and then we started that sweet rolling until the both of us were screaming as if the last piece of love was dying forever. After that, we just laid there, talking soft up into the air. I would tell her she was the loveliest bitch that ever lived, and all of a sudden she was no longer calling me a dirty mother-fucker, she was calling me a sweet mother-fucker. It got quiet. I sat up on the edge of the bed with my head hanging long and deep, trying to push myself out of the room and back into it at one and the same time. She looked up at me and I got that same question all over again. Will you marry me and be the father of your son! I tried to move away from her, but she dug her fingernails into my shoulders. I struck her once, twice, and again and again—with this hand! And her face was a bloody mess! And I felt real bad about that. I said, I'll marry you, *Yes! Yes! Yes!*

(*Pause.*)

I put my clothes on and I walked out into the streets, trembling with the knowledge that now I have a little boy who I must walk through the park with every Sunday, who one day just may blow my head off—and an abiding wife who on a given evening may get herself caught in the bed of some other man, and I could be sealed in a dungeon until dead! I was found lying in a well of blood on the day I was born! But I have been kind! I have kissed babies for the simple reason they were babies! I'm going to get married to some bitch and that gets me to shaking all over! (*He moves close to* THEO.) The last time I trembled this way *I killed a man!* (*Quickly and rhythmically takes out a long, shiny switchblade knife. It pops open just at* THEO's *neck.* BLUE *holds it there for a moment, then withdraws and closes it. Puts it away. Then he collects his belongings, then calmly addresses* THEO.) Things are tight and cool on my end, Theo, and that's how you should keep it here. If not, everything gets messy and I find myself acting like a policeman, keeping order. I don't have the time for that kind of trick. (BLUE *exits.*)

THEO

(*After a moment of silent thought, moves decisively to the back-room stairs and calls.*) Bobby! (BOBBY *comes downstairs.*)

THEO

I want you to stay away from those store raids, Bobby.

BOBBY

Not as long as I can get myself some extra money. (*Moving close to him.*) You didn't say nothing to me before, when I was stealing every other day and giving you half of everything I stole. You didn't think nothing that day you sent me for that typewriter!

THEO

I don't know what you're going to do from here on in, because I'm calling the whole affair off with Blue.

BOBBY

That won't stop me, and you know it!

THEO

What is it, Bobby—we used to be so close! Bobby, don't get too far away from me!

BOBBY

(*Heatedly.*) What do you want me to do? Stick around you all the time? Hell, I'm tired of you! I stick by you and I don't know what to do! I steal and that puts clothes on my back and money in my pockets! *That's* something to do! But I sit here with you all day just thinking about the next word I'm going to say—I'm not stupid! I sit here all day thinking about what I'm going to say to you. I stuck by you and I hoped for you because whatever you became, I was gonna become. I thought about that, and that ain't shit! (*He leaves the shop.* THEO *is alone with his troubled thoughts. Suddenly he rushes into back room, gets hat and shirt, puts them on, and goes out into the street.*)

MR. PARKER

(*Stepping down into the back room from the apartment upstairs.*) Come on, girl! (*A very attractive, well-dressed* YOUNG GIRL *in her early twenties follows him into the shop.*)

MR. PARKER

You wanted to see it. Well, here it is.

GIRL

(*Looking about the place.*) So this is where you do your business. Like I keep asking you, Russell, what kind of business is it for you to make all that money you got?

MR. PARKER

(*Heading toward the refrigerator in the back room.*) Come on in here, sweetheart. I'll fix us a drink!

GIRL

(*Moves briskly after him.*) I asked you a question, Russell.

MR. PARKER

(*Still ignoring her question, he takes a jug out of refrigerator and grabs two glasses.*) I'm going to make you a special drink, made from my own hands. It's called "Black Lightning."

GIRL

(*Surveys the room as* PARKER *pours drink.*) That should be exciting.

MR. PARKER

Here you go. (*Hands her the drink.*) *Toujours l'amour!*

GIRL

(*Gasping from the drink.*) What the fuck is this! What *is* this, Russell?

MR. PARKER

(*Patting her on the back.*) Knocks the tail off of you, don't it! But it gets smoother after the second swallow . . . Go on, drink up!

GIRL

Okay. (*Tries it again and scowls. Moves away as he sits on bed.*)

MR. PARKER

Now, did you think about what I asked you last night?

GIRL

About getting married?

MR. PARKER

Yes.

GIRL

Why do you want to marry me, Russell?

MR. PARKER

Because I love you, and I think you could make me happy.

GIRL

Well, I don't believe you. When I asked you a question about your business, you deliberately ignored me. It was like you didn't trust me, and I thought that love and trust went together.

MR. PARKER

I'm not so sure about that. My son Theo, I'm wild about him, but I wouldn't trust him no farther 'n I could throw a building.

GIRL

I'm not your son!

MR. PARKER

What is it you wanta know?

GIRL

Where you gettin' all that money from?

MR. PARKER

Oh, that. That's not for a girl to know, baby doll.

GIRL

Then it's time for me to go. I'm not gettin' myself hooked up with no mystery man! (*Moves as if to leave.* PARKER *stops her, then pauses for a moment.*)

151

MR. PARKER

All right, I'll tell you. I'm partners in a big business, which I'm the president of.

GIRL

Partners with who, Russell?

MR. PARKER

That's not important, baby.

GIRL

Partners with who, Russell.

MR. PARKER

Mr. Blue Haven.

GIRL

Blue Haven! Then it's crooked business.

MR. PARKER

Oh no, baby, it's nothing like that. It's real straight

GIRL

What does that mean?

MR. PARKER

That what we're doing is right!

GIRL

Tell me about it, then.

MR. PARKER

I've said enough. Now let's leave it at that! (*Tries to embrace her.*)

GIRL

(*Wards him off, sits on bed.*) All you take me for is something to play with.

MR. PARKER

That's not true, I wanna marry you. (*Sits beside her.*)

GIRL

You say you want to marry me, but how do you expect me to think about marrying somebody who won't confide in me about what they're doing. How do I know I'm not letting myself in for trouble.

MR. PARKER

(*Ponders for a moment, then rises.*) All right, I'll tell you! We peddle a variety of products to the community and we sell things to people at a price they can't get nowhere else in this city. Yes, according to the law it's illegal, but we help our people, our own people. We take care of business and at the same time we make everybody happy. We take care of our people. Just like I been taking care of you.

153

GIRL

You take care of me? How? You've never given me more than ten dollars in cash since I've known you.

MR. PARKER

Well, I've got a big present for you coming right out of this pocket and I'm gon' take you downtown tomorrow and let you spend till the store runs out.

GIRL

Taking me to a store and giving me spending change makes me feel like a child and I don't like it and I'm not gonna stand for it any more.

MR. PARKER

Then take this and you do whatever you want with it.

GIRL

(*Taking the money and putting it away.*) Now don't get the idea I'm just in love with your money.

MR. PARKER

Now I want you to stop talking to me about money. I've got *plenty* of it! You've got to understand—I'm the most different man you ever met. I've been around this world, I danced before the King and Queen of England. I've seen and heard many a thing in my lifetime—and you know what: I'm putting it all down on paper—my story!

GIRL

Your story!

(MR. PARKER *moves into shop, gets notebook from behind one of the sliding panels. During his absence* GIRL *checks under the bed.*)

MR. PARKER

(*Re-enters.*) Here it is, right here. (*Sits next to her on the bed, giving her the notebook.*)

GIRL

(*Thumbing through the pages.*) You write things too?

MR. PARKER

I certainly do—and I've been thinking about writing a poem about you.

GIRL

A poem about me!

MR. PARKER

(*Taking book from her and dropping it on floor.*) I'm gon' do it tonight before I go to sleep. (*He kisses her neck and reaches for the hem of her dress.*)

GIRL

(*Breaking out of his embrace.*) No, Russell, not here!

MR. PARKER

Why not?

GIRL

Just because there's a bed wherever we go don't mean that we have to jump into it. You don't understand, Russell! You've got to start treating me the same as if I was your wife.

MR. PARKER

That's exactly what I'm trying to do!

GIRL

(*Rising.*) Don't yell at me!

MR. PARKER

All right. I tell you what: I'm kinda tired, let's just lie down for a while and talk. I ain't gon' try nothing.

GIRL

Russell—

MR. PARKER

May the Lord smack me down this minute into hell—I swear I won't do nothing.

GIRL

What are the three biggest lies men tell to women, Russell?

MR. PARKER

I ain't just any man—I'm the man you gon' spend your life with.

GIRL

Okay, Russell, we'll lie down, but you've got to keep your word. If I'm the girl you want to marry, you've got to learn to keep your word. (*They lie on bed. To her surprise,* PARKER *is motionless, seemingly drifting off to sleep. After a moment she takes the initiative and begins love-making. He responds, and once his passion has reached an aggressive peak she breaks off abruptly.*) Where do you get these things you sell to people?

MR. PARKER

What are you talking about?

GIRL

You know what I'm saying. I overheard you tell Mr. Jenkins you suspected your son was robbing stores.

MR. PARKER

You heard no such thing!

GIRL

(*Desperately.*) Where do they keep the stuff?

MR. PARKER

Now, baby, you've got to relax and stop worrying about

things like that! (*Pulls her by the shoulders. She does not resist.*) Come here. (*He pulls her down to the bed, takes her into his arms and kisses her, reaching again for the hem of her dress.*)

GIRL

(*Struggling, but weakening to his ardor.*) Russell, you said you wouldn't do nothing!

MR. PARKER

I ain't! I just want to get a little closer to you!

GIRL

Russell, not here!

MR. PARKER

Just let me feel it a little bit!

GIRL

You swore to God, Russell! (THEO *comes in the front door and heads toward back room.*)

MR. PARKER

I ain't gon' do nothing!

GIRL

(*Hears* THEO.) Russell! Russell! Somebody is out there!

MR. PARKER

(*Jumps up quickly.* THEO *stands before him.*) What are you doing here?

THEO

The question is, *what are you doing!*

MR. PARKER

I have been having a private talk with a good friend of mine. Now get out of here!

(GIRL *jumps up, moving past* MR. PARKER.)

MR. PARKER

(*Stopping her.*) Where are you going?

GIRL

Home!

MR. PARKER

Hold it now, honey!

GIRL

I never should have come here in the first place!

MR. PARKER

No, you're not going anywhere. This is my place and you don't have to run off because of this Peeping Tom!

159

THEO

Pop, it's time to give us our money.

MR. PARKER

You'll get your share tomorrow and not before!

THEO

I want it now before you give it all to that girl. Pop, cut that broad loose!

MR. PARKER

What was that?

THEO

I said, cut her loose! She don't need an old man like you, she's just pumping you for information. That bitch is a hustler!

MR. PARKER

(*Slaps* THEO *with the back of his hand.*) Bite your tongue!

GIRL

I think I better go, Russell. (*Heads for the front door.*)

MR. PARKER

(*Following her.*) Okay, but I'll be right with you as soon as I get things straight here. You will be waiting for me, won't you?

160

GIRL

Sure!

MR. PARKER

You run along now and I'll be right over there. (GIRL *exits.* PARKER *whirls back into shop.*) What do you think you're doing, boy?

THEO

Just be careful, Pop. Please be careful.

MR. PARKER

If there's anybody I got to be careful of, it's you! You lying selfish sonofabitch! You think I don't know about you and Blue running that gang of thieves—about you sending your own brother out there with them?

THEO

I didn't do that!

MR. PARKER

If Bobby gets hurt out on them streets, I'm gonna kill you, boy! I'm gonna kill you. (*Hurriedly collects hat and coat.*)

THEO

You're not worried about Bobby! All you can think of is the money you're rolling in. The clothes. And that stupid outfit you've got on.

(ADELE *comes in from the street, obviously distraught.*)

MR. PARKER

What's wrong with you? Are you drunk? (*Moves in.* ADELE *doesn't answer, so he moves off.*)

THEO

Of course she's drunk. What did you expect—did you think everything would stop and stand still while you were being reborn again!

MR. PARKER

What do you want from me? Call this whole thing off? It was your idea, not mine! But now that I've got myself something—I'm not going to throw it away for nobody!

THEO

But can't you see what's happening here?

MR. PARKER

If she wants to be a drunken wench, let her! I'm not going to take the blame. And as for you— (*Fumbles in his coat pocket.*) If you want this money, you can take it from me—I can throw every dollar of it into the ocean if I want to! You can call me a fool too, but I'm a *burning fool!* I'm going to marry that little girl. She is not a whore! She is a woman! And I'm going to marry her! And if the two of you don't like it, you can kiss my ass! (*Bolts out into the street.*)

THEO

You're not drunk. What happened?

ADELE

(*Heading for the back room.*) What does it look like. Wilmer hit me.

THEO

(*Following.*) Why?

ADELE

(*Sits on bed.*) He caught me in Morgan's with a friend of his after I had lied about going bowling with the girls. He just walked in and started hitting me, over and over again. His friend just stood there pleading with him not to hit me, but he never did anything to stop him. I guess he figured, "Why should I risk getting myself killed over just another piece of ass?" I thought he was going to kill me but then Blue came in with some of his friends and they just grabbed him by the arms and took him away.

THEO

Was Bobby with them?

ADELE

I couldn't tell.

THEO

Damnit! Everything gets fucked up!

ADELE

It had to, because you don't think. If you're going to be a crook, you don't read a comic book for research, you don't recruit an old black man that's about to die!

THEO

No matter what you do, he's gon' die anyway. This whole place was built for him to die in—so you bite, you scratch, you kick: you do anything to stay alive!

ADELE

Yes, you bite! You scratch, you steal, you kick, and you get killed anyway! Just as I was doing, coming back here to help Momma.

THEO

Adele, I'm sick and tired of your talk about sacrifices. You were here because you had no other place to go. You just got scared too young and too soon.

ADELE

You're right. All I was doing was waiting for her to die so I could get on with what I thought I wanted to do with myself. But, God, *she took so long to die!* But then I found myself doing the same things she had done, taking care of three men, trying to shield them from the danger beyond that door, *but who the hell ever told every black woman she was some kind of goddamn savior!* Sure, this place was built for us to die in, but if we aren't very careful, Theo—that can actually happen. Good night. (*Heads for the stairs.*)

THEO

Adele— (*She stops in her tracks and turns.*) I've decided that there's going to be no more of Blue's business here. It's over. We're getting out.

ADELE

(*After a long pause.*) Theo, do you really mean it? (THEO *nods yes.*)

ADELE

What about Daddy?

THEO

He will have to live with it. This set-up can't move without me.

ADELE

And Bobby?

THEO

I'll take care of him.

ADELE

That's fine, Theo. We'll throw the old things into the river —and we'll try something new: I won't push and you won't call me a bitch! (*Goes upstairs.* THEO *picks up his*

*father's notebook from the floor beside the bed. A knock
at the door.*)

THEO

    We're closed!

(*The knocking continues.*)

THEO

    WE'RE CLOSED!

(*The knocking turns to banging and a voice calls out to*
THEO. *He rushes to the door and opens.*)

THEO

    I SAID WE'RE CLOSED! Oh, I'm sorry, Mr. Jenkins, I
didn't know that was you . . . What are you doing here
this time of night?

MR. JENKINS

    I want to speak to Parker.

THEO

    You know him—he's been keeping late hours lately. . .

MR. JENKINS

    I'll wait for him.

THEO

Suit yourself, but don't you have to work tomorrow?

MR. JENKINS

I have something to tell him, and I'll wait if it takes all night.

THEO

In that case, you can tell me about it.

(ADELE *comes downstairs and stops on steps leading to shop, looking about confusedly. She has a deadly, almost blank look on her face.*)

THEO

What's wrong with you?

ADELE

(*Pause.*)
Some—somebody just called me.

THEO

What did they call you about? (*She does not answer.* JENKINS *rises and seats her gently on bed.*) Didn't you hear me—what about? (*She still does not respond.*) WHAT IS IT, ADELE!!!

MR. JENKINS

THEO!!! (THEO *turns to* MR. JENKINS.) I think she probably just heard that your brother Bobby has been killed in a robbery by a night watchman.

THEO

Uh-uh, nawww, nawww, that's not true.

MR. JENKINS

Yes, it is, son.

ADELE

Yes.

THEO

No.

MR. JENKINS

Yes! (*Moves toward the shop door.*)

THEO

I don't believe you!

MR. JENKINS

I saw him, boy, I saw him. (*Dead silence as* MR. JENKINS *slowly moves toward the street exit.*)

THEO

You should've seen this dude I caught the other day on Thirty-second Street. He had on a bright purple suit, gray shirt, yellow tie, and his hair was processed with bright purple color. What a sight he was! But I have to say one thing for him—he was clean. (*The lights are slowly dimming.*) Used to be a time when a dude like that came in numbers, but you don't see too many of them nowadays. I have to say one thing for him—he was clean. You don't see too many like—he was clean. He was—he was clean—

BLACKOUT

SCENE TWO

About two hours later, in the shop.

MR. PARKER *and* MR. JENKINS *enter the shop.* MR. PARKER *is drunk, and* MR. JENKINS *helps him walk and finally seats him on the barber's throne.*

MR. PARKER

Thank you, Jenkins. You are the greatest friend a man can have. They don't make 'em like you any more. You are one of the last of the great friends, Jenkins. Pardon me, Mister Jenkins. No more will I ever call you Jenks or Jenkins. From now on, it's Mister Jenkins!

MR. JENKINS

Thank you, but when I ran into Theo and Adele tonight,

they said they had something important to say to you, and
I think you oughta see them.

MR. PARKER

I know what they want. They want to tell me what an
old fool I am.

MR. JENKINS

I don't think that's it, and you should go on upstairs
and—

MR. PARKER

Never! Upstairs is for the people upstairs!

MR. JENKINS
Russell, I—

MR. PARKER

I am downstairs people! You ever hear of downstairs
people?

MR. JENKINS
(*Pause.*)
No.

MR. PARKER
Well, they're the people to watch in this world.

172

MR. JENKINS
If you say so.

MR. PARKER
Put your money on 'em!

MR. JENKINS
Come on, Mister Parker: why don't you lie down in the
back room and—

MR. PARKER
Oh! No—you don't think I'd have you come all the way
over here just for me to go to bed, do you? I wouldn't do
a thing like that to you, Jenkins. I'm busy—Mister Jenkins. Just stay with me for a little while . . . (*His tone
changes.*) Why did that girl lock me out? She said she
would be waiting for me, but she locked me out. Why did
she do a thing like that? I give her everything—money,
clothes, pay her rent. I even love her!

MR. JENKINS
Russell—

MR. PARKER
(*Rising precariously.*) Tell me something, Mister Jenkins
—since you are my friend—why do you think she locked
me out?

173

MR. JENKINS

(*Steadying him.*) I don't know.

MR. PARKER

I'll tell you why. I'm an old man, and all I've got is a few dollars in my pocket. Ain't that it?

MR. JENKINS

I don't know . . . Good night, Parker. (*Starts out.*)

MR. PARKER

(*Grabs his arm.*) You think a man was in that room with my girl?

MR. JENKINS

Yes!

MR. PARKER

Goddamnit! Goddamnit!

MR. JENKINS

Russell—

MR. PARKER

I don't believe it! When I love 'em, they stay loved!

MR. JENKINS

Nobody's got that much love, man!

174

MR. PARKER

(*Pause.*)

No, no—you're wrong. My wife—my dear Doris had more love in her than life should've allowed. A hundred men couldn't have taken all that love.

MR. JENKINS

We ain't talking about Doris, Russell.

MR. PARKER

Aw, forget it! (*Crossing toward table.*) *Goddamnit!* You stumble around like an old black cow and you never get up again . . .

I have had my fun!
If I don't get well no more!
I have had my fun!
If I—

(PARKER *falls down.*) Get up, old bastard! Get up! (*Rises to his feet, aided by* JENKINS.) Get up and fall back down again. Come on, Mister Jenkins, let's play ourselves a game of checkers.

MR. JENKINS

I don't want to play no damn checkers.

MR. PARKER

Why do you curse my home, Mister Jenkins?

MR. JENKINS

(*Pause.*)

I apologize for that.

MR. PARKER

Come on, have a game of checkers with your good friend.
(*Sits at table.*)

MR. JENKINS

(*Moves to the table.*) All right, one game and then I'm
going home.

MR. PARKER

One game.

MR. PARKER

(*Pausing while* JENKINS *sits down.*) I said a lot of dirty
things to my children tonight—the kind of things you
have to live a long time to overcome.

MR. JENKINS

I know exactly what you mean. (JENKINS *sets up jumps
for* PARKER. PARKER *seems unaware of it. They play
briefly.* PARKER *stops.*)

MR. PARKER

Theo is a good boy, and a smart one too, but he lets people push him around. That's because he's always trying to
con somebody out of something—you know the kind:
can't see for looking. And Bobby? He wouldn't hurt a
flea. A lot of people think that boy is dumb, but just let
somebody try to trick or fool him if they dare! (*Begins
a series of checker jumps.*)

(*Pause.*)

Got a story for you.

MR. JENKINS

No stories tonight, Parker . . .

MR. PARKER

Mister Parker. (*The last move is made, the game is over.
His conquest slowly sinks in. And* MR. PARKER *is at long
last the victor. Rising from the table.*) Call me champ!
(THEO *and* ADELE *enter shop from outside, and stand
just inside the door.* PARKER *is laughing.*) You're beat! I
beat you! I beat you! (MR. PARKER *throws his arm around*
MR. JENKINS'*s waist and holds him from behind.*) . . .
You fall down and you never get up! (*Still laughing.*)
Fall down, old man! Fall down! (*Releases* JENKINS *upon
seeing* ADELE *and* THEO.) You hear that, children, I beat
him! I beat him! (*His laughter subsides as he realizes they*

are not responding to him. Guilt-ridden, he approaches THEO, *looks at him intently, then reaches into his inside coat pocket and pulls out the money.*) Here, Theo, here's the money, here's all of it. Take it, it's yours. Go out and try to get happy, boy. (THEO *does not move or take the money from his father's outstretched hand. He turns to* ADELE. *Her face is almost a blank.*) WHY DON'T SOMEBODY SAY SOMETHING! (ADELE *attempts to speak but* PARKER *cuts her off.*) I know you have some trouble with me . . . (PARKER *spies the notebook in the throne, takes it in his hand, and approaches* ADELE.) You have a woman, you love her, you stop loving her, and sooner or later she ups and dies and you sit around behaving like you was a killer. I didn't have no more in me. I just didn't have no more in me!

(*Pause.*)

I know you don't believe I ever loved your mother, but it's here in this book—read it . . . (*She does not respond.*) You wanta read something, boy! (THEO *turns away.* PARKER *slowly crosses, hands the book to* MR. JENKINS, *and addresses his remarks to him.*) I got sour the day my legs got so trembly and sore on the stage of the Strand Theatre—I couldn't even walk out to take a proper bow. It was then I knew nobody would ever hire me to dance again. I just couldn't run downtown to meet the man the way she did—not after all those years of shuffling around like I was a dumb clown, with my feet hurting and aching the way they did, having my head patted as if I was some little pet animal: back of the bus, front of the train, grinning when I was bleeding to death! . . . After all of that I was going to ask for more by throwing myself into the low drag of some dusty old factory in Brooklyn. All I could do was to stay here in this shop with you, my good friend. And we acted out the ceremony of a game. And you, boy— (*Turns to* THEO.) . . . You and Blue with your ideas of overcoming the evil of white men. To an old man like me, it was nothing more than an ounce of time to end my dragging about this shop. All it did was to send me out into those streets to live a time—and I did live myself a time for a while. I did it amongst a bunch of murderers—all kinds of 'em—where at times it gets so bad till it seems that the only thing that's left is for you to go out there and kill somebody before they kill you. That's all—that's out there! (*Goes to* ADELE.) Adele, as for that girl that was here tonight, she's probably no good, but if at my age I was stupid enough to think that I could have stepped out of here and won that little girl, loved her, and moved through the rest of my days without kill- ing anybody, that was a victory! (*Moves to center stage, stands silently, then does a little dance.*) Be a dancer—any kind of dancer you wanta be—but dance it! (*Tries out a difficult step, but can't quite make it.*) Uh-uhhh! Can't make that one no more. (*Continues to dance.*) Be a singer —sing any song you wanta sing, but sing! (*Stops in his tracks.*) *And you've got enough trouble to take you to the graveyard!*

179

(*Pause.*)

But think of all that life you had before they buried you. (*Breaks into a frantic dance, attempting steps that just cross him up. He stumbles about until he falls. Everyone in the room rushes to help him up.*) . . . I'm okay, I'm okay . . . (*He rises from the floor, slowly.*) I'm tired, I'm going to bed and by the time tomorrow comes around, let's see if we can't all throw it into the river. (*Moves into the back room, singing.*)

> I have had my fun!
> If I don't get well no more
> I have had my fun
> If I don't get well no more—

(*A thought strikes him. He turns and moves back to where* JENKINS *is standing at the entrance to the back room.*) Jenkins, you said that the day I beat you playing checkers, you said it could be the unluckiest day of my life. But after all that's happened today—I'm straight—I feel just great! (*Moves to the stairs leading up, suddenly stops, turns and briskly moves back to the doorway leading to the shop.*) Say, where's Bobby?

CURTAIN